PASTOR & STAFF
SEARCH COMMITTEE GUIDE

DON R. MATHIS

Convention Press

Nashville, Tennessee

ISBN 0-7673-9127-6

Dewey Decimal Classification: 254

Subject Heading: PASTOR SEARCH COMMITTEE / CHURCH ADMINISTRATION

Printed in the United States of America.

Unless otherwise noted, all Scripture quotations are from the Holy Bible,
New International Version, copyright © 1973, 1978, 1984 by International Bible Society.

Pastor-Staff Leadership Department
The Sunday School Board of
the Southern Baptist Convention
127 Ninth Avenue, North
Nashville, Tennessee 37234

CONTENTS

INTRODUCTION

Sooner or later every church must deal with the matter of finding God's man to be the church's next pastor. And many churches, working with their pastor, will from time to time need a systematic process for calling a staff minister. The whole search process can be one of the most rewarding or frustrating experiences in the life of the church. The decisions that are made have consequences far into the future. In fact, the calling of a pastor is likely the most important decision a church makes. The calling of a staff minister does not rank far behind. Therefore, the process must be approached prayerfully and systematically with determination that in every step of the way the will of God will be ascertained and done.

Chapter One

CALLING A
STAFF MINISTER

The calling of staff ministers—whatever the particular title: associate pastor, minister of music, administration, education, recreation, youth, or combination of responsibilities—is to be approached with the same seriousness and seeking of the will of God as in the calling of a pastor. Some churches find it helpful to focus on the functions of the church even in the title of the minister—worship, evangelism, discipleship, ministry, and fellowship.[1] This has advantages, including the recognition of each minister as a minister first and foremost who is exercising his gifts according to the provisions and the calling of God. Unique issues to consider when seeking individuals for specific staff ministry positions are included in the appendix along with sample job descriptions.

Is the process of calling a pastor and a staff minister the same? There are similarities, and yet there are a number of differences. The most significant difference is that the pastor is being called to lead the staff, and the staff minister is being called to work for and/or alongside of the pastor. In calling "staff," the church is looking for someone whose philosophy of ministry, whose personality, whose giftedness, and whose experience complement that of the pastor. Nothing can be more joyful than the right staff mix. Nothing can be more difficult than working with a staff who have competing philosophies.

In addition to complementary philosophies, complementary personalities are important. Many studies have been done to determine the best personality mixes. These studies also reveal ways that different personalities can learn to work with and appreciate other individuals' strengths and weaknesses. A compatible mix of spiritual giftedness can strengthen the staff as a team with each bringing certain strengths and offsetting one another's weaknesses. For example, a staff minister with the gift of administration may be just what a pastor needs if his gift(s) are in teaching, prophecy, or mercy. On the other hand, if the pastor and the staff minister are similarly gifted, duplication of effort and even competition can develop.

A church calling a staff member needs to clarify a prospective staff person's job expectations. Who is going to supervise whom? What are the expectations of the position? What results are being sought? How will this person know when he is succeeding or meeting expectations? These matters, dealt with before the call is made, are essential.

How can a compatible, successful staff be put together? Prayer is not to be an afterthought. Invite God to guide at the beginning and step-by-step throughout the process. Take time to listen, observe, and determine where and in whom He is working. This cannot be overemphasized in bringing a team together.

In ongoing ministry roles mutual respect for one another's ministries is an absolute essential for a church's leadership team. With a sincere desire for the Holy Spirit's leadership, the individuals who must work closely together should spend much time together sharing dreams, insights, and convictions as the will of God is sought in every aspect of the church's ministries.

These realities make calling a staff minister unique from calling a pastor. At the forefront of the differences is the deep involvement of the pastor in the calling of a staff minister. In this book, when the calling of the staff minister is different from that of the pastor, it will be so noted. But for the sake of simplicity, most of the references in the book will be to the calling of a pastor.

---

[1] Gene Mims, *Kingdom Principles for Church Growth* (Nashville: Convention Press, 1994), 9.

Chapter Two

FINDING AN INTERIM PASTOR

With the leaving of a pastor, deep emotions are inevitably involved, and feelings are highly sensitized. Seldom does the church need to call a new pastor immediately. An interim time allows the church to evaluate itself, refocus, and work through any remnants of the past. This does not apply only to the close of an unhappy pastoral era. Often, when a pastor's tenure has marked a very good time in the life of the church, an interim is needed even more. The previous pastor may have retired, died, or moved to another church. The church may feel that it is giving up a large portion of its life if the pastor's stay has been long and/or his impact has been substantial. The church may feel rejected if the stay were short or the pastor went to a larger church. Dreams for the future may be shattered by the pastor's leaving. The church may feel guilty over treatment of the former pastor. All sorts of situations, as unique as each individual church, exist. Even among the best of these, an interim pastor is often a good idea.

WHOM SHOULD A CHURCH NOT CALL AS INTERIM?

A pitfall to be avoided is the inclination to call the immediate past pastor as interim. This may seem like a logical action when a beloved pastor reaches retirement, will continue in the area, and is available to continue preaching. The inherent dangers are many. There may be little actual change between his former role a pastor and his new role as interim. Because the church feels that it still has a pastor, the search committee may move slower than it should. The situation is ready-made for the former pastor to be overly active in the search process. When a new pastor is called, it may be difficult for him to have immediate fellowship with the people, a necessary ingredient for church health.

For many of the same reasons, an associate pastor should, in most cases, not be the interim pulpit minister. In addition, there is the danger that he or the people will get too comfortable with this role. History provides abundant illustrations where the associate and/or people have openly or secretly manipulated attempts to make the associate pastor the permanent pastor. Even when this fails, it is difficult for him to relinquish leadership to the pastor when a new one is called.

Only when the associate requests consideration as a senior-pastor candidate should such consideration occur. When such is the case, he needs to be the first person considered. Obviously, if he is not chosen as pastor, he must of necessity be prepared to move from the church in preparation for the church's proceeding with the normal process for calling a pastor. All of these factors make the calling of an associate as interim pulpit minister a matter that, if done, must be approached with extreme caution.

Many of these same principles apply not only to the senior pastor but to all other ministerial staff positions as well. When a pastor or staff minister resigns, the congregation needs time to grieve—whatever the reason for the resignation. This is especially true when the resignation is of the pastor. This can occur best with an interim who has not in the immediate past been a part of the church's leadership team.

WHERE CAN A CHURCH FIND AN INTERIM?

Often retired pastors, missionaries, and chaplains are available to serve as interims. Depending on location and the logistics of travel, seminary and college professors, employees of a convention agency and institutions on either the state or national level make good interims. Often the director of associational missions can serve on a limited basis as an interim. In any case he and the director of minister relations of the state convention can help in this process as well as in the whole pastor search process.

WHAT IS THE ROLE OF AN INTERIM?

The role of interim pastors varies depending on the needs of the church and the gifts, experience, and available time of the interim minister. Obviously, the proclamation of the gospel must continue even though the church is pastorless. When the same person is in the pulpit week after week, this consistency enhances the hearing of the message.

An effective interim pastor can promote fellowship through his preaching, his personality, and insights developed from past experiences. In some cases, he can give time to counseling and hospital and other forms of personal visitation. It is often wise that he give leadership to the staff. This is preferred to one of the staff ministers being appointed to be in charge, which may lead to confusion over authority after the new pastor comes. Also disharmony can result when one peer minister finds himself suddenly thrust into the position of answering to another minister of the same staff rank.

The interim pastor can be a real source of counsel for the search committee. However, caution should be used to ensure that the interim does not influence the church toward calling a person he handpicks.

The greatest value of an interim pastor may be that his presence can take pressure off the search committee to rush toward calling a pastor. He can provide stability, continuity, and security for the church and the committee, while allowing the search committee to be prayerful and patient in the search process.

How should a church go about finding an interim pastor? Actually the process is not unlike that of finding a permanent pastor. The primary difference is that the process is not typically as intense, since it is temporary.

WHO IS TO FIND THE INTERIM?

The assignment of securing an interim can be given to the pastor search committee. This plan offers some advantages. Communication lines are open from the beginning to allow the interim to be in a better position gradually to move the church toward the point of being ready for a new pastor in concert with the timing of the committee. It also gives the committee a mini-trial run in the procedures of a search process.

On the other hand, there are certain advantages of an interim search committee. This committee can be single focused. Also this makes it less likely that the interim will dominate or influence the pastor search process in an unhealthy way. In this case, the deacons, a subcommittee of the deacons, a committee nominated by the nominating committee, the Church Council, or a committee elected from the floor can appropriately serve. In any case, this committee should be elected by the church and their recommendation acted on by the church.

ARE THERE DIFFERENT KINDS OF INTERIMS?

Some churches today benefit from what is called an intentional interim. This process essentially is the signing of a contract with a specially trained interim who will give leadership to the church over an extended period of time. This is to be an intentional time of dealing with long-term problems, attending to deep hurts, or refocusing of necessities. If this is of interest, many state conventions can be helpful and will be glad to give guidance.

Most churches continue to choose a *transitional interim*. In this model, the interim sees himself and is seen by the church as providing stability and limited leadership for the church as the church begins and continues its journey toward finding a new pastor. In this role, the interim is simply building a bridge between pastors.

It is almost always best that the church be assured that the interim is not a candidate to be permanent pastor. Occasionally an interim has been called as pastor with good results, but in most cases it has been divisive. When this happens, the work of the search committee is circumvented by some other group of strong, vocal members bypassing policy, usually to the spoken or silent resistance of others. Even on some occasions the interim has taken advantage of the vulnerability of the church to force his way in as pastor. The results can be disastrous.

A written agreement between the church and the interim pastor is a good policy. This can be a simple statement of expectations and compensation. It can even contain a covenant stating that the interim will not be a candidate for pastor and that the church will not try to persuade otherwise. This document can prevent later misunderstanding.

Chapter Three

SELECTING
A SEARCH
COMMITTEE

Autonomous churches select pastor and staff search committees in a variety of ways. Usually this is spelled out in the church's constitution and bylaws. When it is, then these guidelines should, of course, be followed to the letter.

If the church does not have a constitution and bylaws or does not have within it clear guidelines, the time without a pastor is not a good time to deal with constitution and bylaw matters. It is usually best, under the leadership of the Church Council, deacons, or a similar group to work with the moderator in preparing a method of selection to be affirmed by the congregation.

Even within adopted guidelines there may be room for flexibility. When this is true, decisions need to be made carefully regarding procedures. When not well thought out, actions that cure one problem may create another.

Methods vary considerably. There is no right or wrong way to select a search committee, but some methods are better than others. The nominating committee may be responsible for enlisting persons to serve and recommending them to the church. This can be effective if the recommended search committee represents the entire church. The danger is that the search committee will, usually unintentionally, represent only the power structure without good representation of the entire church.

The nominating committee may decide that the church is ready for a new day and may steer clear of past leaders to the extent of electing a committee which is out of touch with who the church really is. The nominating committee can allow one vocal person to persuade an imbalance toward or away from either gender, senior adults, or youth. If this is the method used for choosing or, for that matter, whatever the method of choosing, careful consideration must be taken to allow representation and balance.

The search committee should not overrepresent one economic group, social clique, or family. As much as possible, the search committee ought to be a microcosm of the church.

In some churches the deacons, or a group selected by them from among the deacons, serve as the search committee. This is usually not best. Many segments of the church are usually left out, and the committee likely will fail to involve any newer members of the church.

The church may nominate search committee candidates from the floor during a business meeting. The danger is that more vocal or dominant members may virtually select the entire committee.

Other churches list all members, usually adult members, and ask the church to vote for a given number. This is a better method than the others mentioned so far, but it is likely to spread out the votes in such a way that few, if any, members of the committee actually receive a majority of the votes cast.

Perhaps the best method is for nominations to be accepted during a given time period. Then, from the nominees, the congregation is asked to vote for a certain number. The church will probably want to predetermine that the committee will be composed of at least two women, one person under 18, and one over 60. When the ballots are counted, after the number from each of these categories has been selected, the remaining number will be selected without reference to age or gender. Of course, there could be more than two women elected, more than one person above 60, and more than one youth selected, which would be excellent. However, most often, this method of selection will mean that a committee of seven will be composed of four men and two women (the person above 60 may be male or female) and a youth (who may be male or female). The key is representation of the entire church, as much as possible. Above all, the persons selected should be godly people, committed to the church and willing to diligently seek God's will. This process should be guided by the Church Council, or the council can assign the responsibility to the nominating committee (unless otherwise provided for in the church's constitution and bylaws).

The Optimum Size for the Committee

Committees can be larger than seven, but logistics become more complicated. The larger the group, the more difficult unanimity becomes. A smaller membership church may be well served by a committee of five. Also, if the committee is small, two alternate members may be selected to serve in case one or two of the committee members make a last-minute decision not to serve or during the process must leave the committee for any reason. If this happens, additional alternates need not be selected. Only if the committee, after having added the two alternates, drops below the number specified for a full committee, should extra persons be added to the search committee. If that happens, rather than moving to the person receiving the next highest votes when the selection was held, the nominating committee can be asked to recommend to the church an additional member. This is more likely to maintain a good balance and membership representation on the committee.

Some churches have found it best to elect a specific number of committee members with no alternates. The advantage is the elimination of the ambiguity of roles between members and alternates. The disadvantage is that if committee members must drop out during the search process the committee may be depleted. In this approach, the church might choose to elect nine members, for example, and agree that additional committee members will not be elected unless the number falls below seven.

The Role of the Leaving Pastor

Although the resigning pastor may, if appropriate, help the church to design a method for committee selection, it is unwise for him to participate in the selection of the search committee. He may indeed have shown himself to be an effective and beloved pastor, but he needs to be willing to release the church to a new era.

Each person selected to serve on the committee should be contacted to confirm his/her willingness to serve before any names are announced. At the time the entire committee is announced and presented to the church, an installation may be planned for the congregation to participate in a period of affirmation and prayer. (For further discussion of the installation service see chapter 7, "Encouraging Congregational Input.") The occasion of installation is an excellent time to present each search committee member and alternate with a copy of this book.

Chapter Four

ORGANIZING THE COMMITTEE

The search committee has been selected, enlisted, announced, and elected by the church. What happens next? Immediately the committee should begin to organize itself.

A good way to begin is for the chairman of the nominating committee, or whoever did the enlisting, to call the search committee's initial meeting. If alternate committee members have been selected, they should attend. Once basic matters have been covered, including the election of officers, if a person outside the committee did the convening, he should excuse himself and allow the committee to begin the process of functioning as a unit.

In this initial meeting, the sections of the church's constitution and bylaws relating to the process of pastor or staff selection should be read by the committee in its entirety. Whatever questions arise in this process should be addressed. Some of this may appear to be elementary, but it is better to overdo than risk any misunderstandings of the committee's role.

Each member of the committee should share his or her personal testimony including relationship with Christ, history of involvement in the church, and how each sees the role of committee members. This can be a gigantic step toward a unity of mind and spirit in the committee.

THE ROLE OF SEARCH COMMITTEE OFFICERS

It is best for the committee to select their own officers rather than their being selected or appointed by someone else. This allows the committee to set its direction immediately. The chair, selected first, should be spiritually mature with a high sense of congregational dynamics and history. He or she must be well respected by the whole church as well as by the committee itself. His/her role will include serving as spokesperson for the committee. At times it will be necessary for the chairperson to manage disagreements and even conflict within the committee. Negotiation among diverse members of the committee will require sensitivity and determination. This person must be willing to give even larger amounts of time than will be required of other committee members. These are all significant factors to be considered in selecting the chairman. Especially he or she must be one who walks with God.

Later when the committee begins to contact prospective candidates, the first contact the candidates receive will likely be from the chairperson. Thus, he or she should be a person who makes a good first impression; is able to articulate well the focus of the committee; and is well informed as to the history, convictions, and vision of the church.

The vice chairperson should be similar in gifts and commitment to the chairperson. Responsibilities will include presiding and delegating assignments in the absence of the chairperson.

A recorder is needed who is capable and willing to work hard to maintain minutes of meetings and activities of the committee. This person may also be responsible for keeping a complete file of all profiles, as well as communicating regularly with all candidates. On the other hand, the committee may designate another committee member as the biographical profile coordinator.

A prayer leader may also be selected by the committee with the assignment of monitoring and guiding the spiritual aspects of the process. This will intentionalize the prayer and devotional factors of the search experience rather than just assuming that this most vital factor will automatically happen.

Each meeting should begin with a basic study of the nature of the ministry, with special focus on the particular kind of minister being sought. Many passages relate to the role of the pastor or the gifts and ministry of the staff minister. (Some suggested Scriptures are offered in appendix 1.) A good guide for understanding the leadership role of the pastor or staff minister is *Kingdom Leadership* by Michael Miller.[1] The prayer leader can lead this study or enlist other members of the committee to lead. This should provide a consistent, spiritual focus at the beginning of each meeting.

UNANIMITY

Finding God's will is an absolute nonnegotiable! Open discussion and even disagreements within the committee are to be encouraged. The attitude should be, if you think or feel it, say it—"speaking the truth in love" (Eph. 4:15). Hidden agendas are to be strongly discouraged. Indeed, this is a good time to talk about how disagreements will be handled, including whether the committee must be unanimous before a candidate will be brought before the church. With rare exception, unanimity ought to be the agreed-upon result.

Being unanimous may seem more ideal that realistic, but do not underestimate the ability of the Holy Spirit to lead a group mutually committed to knowing God's will. This does not mean that undue pressure ought to be put on any member of the committee who finds himself or herself in the minority, even if it turns out to be a minority of one.

Each person's convictions must be respected. God may even be at work in this. Examples can be cited of committees that were saved from serious error by the dissenting and persistent vote of one. Does that mean, if such becomes the case, that either the majority or minority ought to be condemned or applauded? No. It may simply mean that God used His revelation to one person to prevent the committee from moving in the wrong direction.

If the search committee is a pastor search committee, it is almost always best for the committee to agree to be unanimous. The exception might be if the committee is extremely large. For example, a 15-member committee might decide that a sufficient consensus has been reached with no more than 1 or 2 negative votes. If this agreement is reached, it ought also to be agreed that such a vote be by secret ballot so that the negative votes will not be identified with particular individuals. Obviously, even with a large committee, unanimity is ideal.

If the search committee is for a minister of education, music, or other staff minister, unanimity may not be as essential. For example, one dissenting vote might not be adequate for not proceeding with a particular candidate. However, the significance of the pastor's vote on the calling of a staff minister cannot be overemphasized. Since he is the person who is assigned the responsibility of leading and supervising the staff, if a person is added to the staff without full support of the pastor, the results are almost always disastrous. The committee must work closely with the pastor to establish a mutual understanding from the beginning as to how agreement on any particular candidate will be reached. A proven approach is that the committee's vote be combined as if it were one vote and the pastor's vote considered one vote. Then all involved in the process should agree that both the committee and the pastor must support the calling of a particular person or they will move on to the next candidate.

FINANCES

In this first meeting the committee should familiarize themselves with financial provision the church has made for the committee's work. Whether a specific amount has been set aside or open-ended authorization has been given, the committee needs to know. Any questions should be noted and clarified before the next meeting with a report given to the group. Most likely the chairperson will want to communicate regarding any questions with the finance committee chairperson, treasurer, or whomever would logically be responsible.

Some members of the search committee cannot afford extra financial expenses themselves. Others can easily provide whatever monies are needed to accomplish the assignment. However, in this responsibility, the committee is acting on behalf of the congregation; therefore, adequate finances should be provided by the church.

The church should be made aware, perhaps through appropriate committees, that the committee's work will certainly involve expenses. Phone calls to profile sources, prospective candidates, and references will need to be made. Many of these will be long-distance and will involve lengthy conversations. Background checks, including financial reports, will certainly need to be done. The committee will need to travel to meet with or hear prospective candidates. This may involve meals, motel bills, gasoline, and perhaps even airfare. There will be meals and other expenses if the committee has a retreat. Certainly, prospective candidates are to be reimbursed for expenses related to dealing with the committee, including travel and lodging for candidates who are invited to visit the church or meet the committee at a neutral location. Cost for tapes or any other incidental expenses should be reimbursed. Good records and receipts will help the committee report expenses.

Additional items that should be dealt with in this first meeting include taking a vow of confidentiality, discussing the role of alternate members (if any), and describing the nuts and bolts of the search process. When these matters have been adequately discussed and agreed upon, the committee should arrange for its next meeting and preliminary plans for regular meetings. The session should close as it began with sincere prayer for God to guide the process.

---

[1] Michael Miller, *Kingdom Leadership: A Call to Christ-centered Leadership* (Nashville: Convention Press, 1996).

Chapter Five

CONDUCTING THE COMMITTEE'S SECOND MEETING

The pastor or staff search committee will find great benefit in making their second meeting a retreat. This can be accomplished in a variety of ways. The committee (and alternates) should be able to give a number of uninterrupted hours to prayer, study, and planning. An entire Saturday might be set aside. Members of the committee can meet at the church, a retreat center, or even a restaurant meeting room. The problem of meeting at the church may be the potential of interruptions. Also, this may in some churches heighten the curiosity of those who discover that the search committee is having a long meeting.

Many committees find that a Saturday, all day, is ideal. Others, simply because of schedules, use a Sunday. This can be done by the members' attending Sunday School and worship as usual, eating a sack lunch, and using the entire afternoon as retreat time.

DEVELOP A KINGDOM PERSPECTIVE

The committee should plan to begin with an overview of *Kingdom Leadership*.[1] (The committee may agree to make this book assigned reading.) This study should not be rushed. An hour might be set aside in this meeting with sections studied in subsequent meetings. There are many benefits of a kingdom perspective. For example, this study will help members understand that God calls out leaders and appoints them to particular places of service at particular times. Often committees feel a bit guilty in going out to "steal" another church's pastor or staff minister. This study will aid in understanding that, if God wants a particular person to give leadership in your church at this particular time, He will also be preparing that person's replacement for his current church. Since God is *the* kingdom leader, He will place His ministers as He sees fit. Our role is to find His will and, also, to help others with whom we are involved to find His will.

Chapter 3, "Jesus Christ: The Leader and His Character," is a basic study of leadership qualifications. It is an essential study for any serious committee. Likewise, chapter 6, "Jesus Christ: The Leader and His Work" will help the committee understand basic skills any leader, pastor, or staff minister must have to be an effective leader. This chapter will help the committee evaluate potential candidates.

Chapter 7, "The Kingdom Leadership Path," may help the committee understand that effective leaders may be at a significant step on the path that would cause them to be open to new opportunities. Also, it will help the committee evaluate the kind of leader they need in light of his progress on the path rather than progress simply based on age, size of congregation served, or number of years in ministry.

In addition, chapter 8, "Kingdom Leadership Life Application," will provide wonderful devotional material for committee meetings.

LET GOD SPEAK THROUGH COMMITTEE MEMBERS

Time should then be taken for the committee to discuss with one another the impressions they individually seem to be receiving from God about the search process. Members might be asked to finish such statements as:

- God seems to be impressing me that the greatest need of our church is _____.

- I feel impressed that what we need in a new pastor is_____.

- If I could say one thing to the rest of the committee, I believe that God would have me say _____.

Many of the responses, indeed perhaps all of the responses, will immediately focus the committee on a need to pray specifically about what has just been said. Times of praying and waiting before the Lord will help provide the prayer atmosphere for the committee to begin or expand its ability to hear from God.

INTENTIONALIZE COMMUNICATION

The third item that ought to be on the retreat agenda is communication. This includes discussion and decisions of communication within the committee, to the church, with individual church members, and with prospective candidates. In addition, where applicable, decisions ought to be made as to how and when other church staff members will be briefed on the committee's progress.

As previously mentioned, all discussions within meetings are to be totally confidential. Even a casual word dropped here or there can be misunderstood, cause rumors to float through the church, or even hurt relationships between a prospective minister (or rumored prospect) and his current place of ministry. Also, more than casual conversation between two or more committee members outside of committee meetings should be guarded to make sure decisions are committee decisions, not those of two or three members done unofficially. The chairperson is the one to whom suggestions from individuals to the committee should flow.

The congregation needs to hear regular reports from the committee—even if no more than informing the church periodically that the committee is meeting, praying, and seeking God's guidance. This is important. The church may be given an open invitation to contribute the names and/or profiles of candidates. When a deadline for receiving recommendations is decided upon, it should be announced to the church well in advance. General reports such as, "We have received many good biographical profiles and are praying over them, evaluating, and investigating" can be helpful. It is also good to be able to say to the church: "The committee is in unity and oneness of spirit. We are excited about the way God is leading us together as a committee."

The congregation should be told that when a member submits a name that member will be unable to track the progress of the recommendation through the search process. Due to the confidential nature of the committee's work, committee members should not give anybody updates on the thinking or the feeling of the committee about any particular candidate. When the point is reached where a person, who knows he was under consideration, has been finally eliminated, the committee should communicate to that person to inform him and to thank him for the opportunity to consider him. Even then, it is usually best not to communicate with the person having made the recommendation but to ask him/her to continue to pray for the committee and to assure him/her that everyone will hear when a recommendation is ready.

Persons eliminated from the search process with whom the committee has not visited should be informed by letter. When the committee has conversations with a particular candidate, if he is eliminated, the more personal touch of a telephone call is appropriate.

When the committee is ready to make a recommendation, every appropriate avenue should be used to communicate the committee's report. Local newspapers, the church's newsletter, bulletins, prayer meetings, worship services, open discussion forums, business meetings, and letters to the church are among the methods that can be used. The committee must be sure to follow to the letter and beyond the requirements of the church's constitution and bylaws. Even if technically not required, the visit in view of a call by a candidate should be announced at least two weeks before the visit. Included should be details as to how the candidate is to be presented, opportunities to meet him, and as many details about the person as possible. Sometimes the initial release may include certain general information about the person and the dates of his consideration without including his name or details that might get back to his present place of service prematurely. Within these and other reasonable precautions, the committee should be as open in communicating with the congregation as possible.

INVOLVE THE STAFF IN THE SEARCH PROCESS

In a multiple-staff church, the search committee should meet with all staff members early in the process to hear their concerns, answer their questions, and receive their suggestions. Certainly the staff is not to do or to circumvent the assignment of the committee; but they can assist one another if they have mutual respect, support, and communication.

Throughout the process, the committee should keep the staff informed as to progress of the search committee. This is especially true if the search is for a pastor. Staff ministers are often understandably anxious as to their own futures when a new pastor is called. Honest reassurance as to confidence they can have in their own situations is good. Then when the search is narrowed, the committee may want to set up a meeting between any serious candidate and the church staff. These meetings can be without public announcement or fanfare at the church or, perhaps better, at a neutral site away from the church. A dinner meeting at a restaurant with the chairman or the entire committee present can be helpful. Sometimes the prospect may want to meet with each staff minister privately, and/or he may want to meet with them as a group. The committee should ask staff ministers to keep these meetings in confidence unless the committee is ready for a public announcement. The committee should be candid with staff ministers as to whether the prospect is one of a group of prospects or he appears to be the choice of the committee. If reaction is expected or sought from a staff minister, obviously, it must be in the strictest confidence. Otherwise, if his reaction is negative and the person is called anyway, he has put himself in a precarious position. In short, treat staff as you would want to be treated if you were in their positions.

In communicating with staff, both staff ministers and support staff should be included. Often support staff, such as a ministry assistant (secretary), may be the person with whom the new pastor or staff minister will work the closest.

DEVELOP A PLAN FOR COMMUNICATING WITH PROSPECTS

The committee should decide early how it will communicate with pastor or staff candidates. Who will speak for the committee? In most cases, it should be the chairperson. If this is the case, it ought to be clearly stated. If another is the official communicator with candidates, that ought to be decided.

Determine at this point that, when profiles are received, a letter acknowledging receipt of information will be sent. Often individuals will eliminate themselves from any consideration. (They may not even be aware that the committee has received their profiles.) From this point, no other letter need be sent unless further information is needed or until and unless the individual is no longer being considered.

PREPARE FOR INTERROGATIONS

Every committee member will be asked many questions. Any or all may even be pressured to reveal confidential information. At times committee members will be aware of "political" activity on behalf of a particular candidate by persons inside or outside the congregation. Committee members may covenant together as a committee not to be forced by human pressure but to be led by the Holy Spirit.

THE MOST VITAL COMMUNICATION IS WITH GOD

Remember that, above all, every committee member must maintain good communication with God through an active devotional life. The search process can be an excellent time for individual growth in learning to listen to God.

---

[1] Michael Miller, *Kingdom Leadership: A Call to Christ-centered Leadership* (Nashville: Convention Press, 1996).

Chapter Six

FINDING THE RIGHT CANDIDATES

Likely, even before the committee has time to meet, organize, pray, and prepare its direction, they will receive profiles of potential ministers. Among those that come unsolicited may be exactly the right person to fill the ministerial position. However, don't assume that everyone who would be open to God's leadership to your church will be among those whose sketches come unsolicited. The committee must be open to taking a proactive approach to find the person God is uniquely preparing for the church at this time.

In discussing the gathering of biographical profiles at this time, it is not to be implied that it is the next recommended step. It is discussed here because it will take time and will be ongoing while the committee is involved in a number of other steps in the search process.

Soon in the committee's meetings the subject of profiles should be addressed. Who will keep the "master file" collection of the profiles. At what point will they be duplicated for other committee members? Where will the committee look to find additional profiles? Who will be assigned which sources to make requests? How long will the committee accept profiles? This last question may not need to be answered until later in the process, but the others need to be answered right away.

Information about possible candidates can be obtained from among the following and other sources.

1. Church members may be asked to give names and perhaps biographical material to the committee.—The committee need not feel that it has to act on every suggestion. On the other hand, the suggestions should be taken seriously. Many ministers can testify of having found God's will for a ministry move as a result of a member's doing something as simple as putting his name on a piece of paper and dropping it in the offering plate. Form and style should not be a criteria, but the more information the member can give on the recommendation the better.

2. Respected ministers often know of persons they can recommend.—This is especially true of those who may be familiar with your church or who have a ministry similar to the kind the committee envisions for the church. I strongly recommend this method of obtaining biographical profiles. Who would better know high-quality ministers than those who themselves are high-quality, godly ministers?

3. Committee members may know of pastors or staff ministers they feel impressed to ask about their interest.—No minister is offended by being asked if he is interested in being considered for a call. If he is not interested, he may share the name of someone with similar gifts and abilities who might be a candidate. Again, many ministers have been led to a particular church through these circumstances.

A word of caution is in order here. If a committee member makes a suggestion, he or she must be willing to let the candidacy of this person be considered only on the same basis as the consideration of any other candidate.

4. The minister relations office (titles vary) of the state convention can be a helpful source, not only for guidance in the search process but with profiles as well.—Indeed, the committee might also contact neighboring state conventions.

5. The director of associational missions (again titles vary) should be a person with whom the committee communicates for insights early in the search process.—Most likely he would be willing to meet with the committee and will have helpful information, sometimes including profiles of potential candidates.

6. Seminaries and Bible colleges through their placement or alumni offices have names and profiles of not only recent graduates but also alumni and others who have attended the school in the past.

7. Other denominational entities, especially those with pastor/staff departments or continuing education opportunities, may have contact with a wide range of persons.

Many of the sources mentioned above will be delighted to share profiles, but they are often not in a position to do background checks and/or may not personally know the persons involved; thus, they are in a position to share information but not make recommendations. In every case, including these, it is imperative that the committee do its own thorough investigations.

Chapter Seven

ENCOURAGING CONGREGATIONAL INPUT

The wise search committee will realize that it represents the congregation. Thus the congregation should be asked to help develop a profile for the prospective new pastor. In some cases this may also be done in a search for a staff minister. The pastor is a generalist with leadership responsibility for the total life and direction of the church, whereas the staff minister is often a specialist with a narrower focus. In either case, whether in a pastor or staff minister search, church participation is vital.

It will be, ultimately, the church's decision whether to call a particular minister. When a call is extended and accepted, the church will be asked to support and follow the new minister. Therefore, the church has both the right and the awesome responsibility for input in the search process. Church input includes:

Prayer support.—As mentioned earlier, the search committee, as it begins its work, should be commissioned by a time of congregational prayer. In many churches this can appropriately be done by the presider (perhaps the moderator, chairman of deacons, nominating committee chairperson, or even the interim pastor) who presents members of the committee to the church. A summary paragraph about each person—how long he or she has been a member, roles in the church, and perhaps a word about the family—will help the congregation in personal prayer support. The congregation may then be invited to gather around the committee for a season of prayer.

A variety of methods may be used to keep a prayer focus before the church during the entire life of the committee. One Sunday a month can be set aside and communicated to the church as prayer day for the committee. If the church has a dial-a-devotion ministry, daily updates can be given at the end of the regular prayer message of the day. Periodic prayer vigils and/or cottage prayer meetings can be conducted. Committee members may enlist prayer partners; caution should be exercised to ensure confidentiality. Special prayer times may also be set during worship services. Magnify the fact that prayer is the highest level of member participation in the search process!

Discovery of what the Bible teaches about pastor and staff leadership.—Ask an appropriate person, perhaps the interim pastor, to lead the committee in an in-depth study of 1 Timothy 3:1-7, Titus 1:4-16, and other appropriate passages. Out of this the committee may feel led to share the study with the entire congregation. After all, more important than what the church and even the committee think or feel about what they want in a pastor or staff minister is what the Bible teaches.

A membership survey.—Most churches and committees find that conducting a survey of the membership can provide helpful information about the congregation and some insights as to what members think they want in a minister. This is especially true for the pastor search committee. Samples of such a survey are available on paper and on disk, for church customization, in *The Pastor and Staff Search Committee Kit.*

The danger of a congregational survey is that it may become a legalistic rule book to the committee. A balanced approach is essential in using survey results. Consider it in looking at potential candidates, but do not allow it to cause the committee to miss God's man simply because his profile may vary a bit from what the members said they wanted. Members may not always understand their real needs at a given time. God may have someone and/or something in mind for the church that the members have not yet envisioned.

Congregational surveys may elevate expectations beyond the reasonable. For example, the same survey may result in the membership desiring a pastor who is 35 years of age with 20 years of pastoral experience. Such a person may exist; but if he does, he probably has not had time to obtain a doctor's degree which may also have been indicated as a congregational desire. Some surveys may go as far as to require that the candidate be married 7.2 years and have 2.3 children. One may get the impression that a pastor must study 20 hours a week yet make every hospital and shut-in visit, lead dozens of persons to salvation every day, attend every church and community event, always be available in his office, and do all of these every week.

Yet, with all of its weaknesses, a survey is a valuable tool. Members need to have input with the search committee and ownership in the process. Indeed, they will want to have input. This is positive because it indicates genuine interest.

With the survey, the simpler and clearer the better! Surveys are often confusing to participants making them of little value to the committee.

Sometimes the committee will do well to mention aspects of the survey. For example, if the congregation indicated a strong desire for evangelism, when a particular candidate is being recommended, the baptism record of the churches he has served might appropriately be emphasized. On the other hand, the chairperson may say in reporting to the church, "We realize that you said in the survey that you wanted a younger pastor. But when we considered Brother _____'s experience and enthusiastic leadership, we felt that the opportunity to call a man of God like him far outweighs age considerations."

Also, the survey can be used to gather factual information about the congregation that will help the committee and the prospective minister. This is assuming that the survey has a section in which participants share information about themselves. Gender, age, education, length of membership, organizations in which they participate, and similar questions can be very helpful.

When should the survey be taken? When the most people will participate. Maximum participation in many churches will occur by taking the survey during Sunday School with each unit being asked to collect them, place them in an envelope, and return them to a committee member. This can be supplemented by including a copy in the church newsletter and making copies available throughout the building to be turned in or mailed in at other times. Of course, a reasonable cutoff time should be announced. The broader the invitation to participate the better. Many churches invite attenders as well as members to participate. If this approach is taken, one of the questions should then allow participants to indicate whether they are members.

The biggest value of the survey may be the partnership and fellowship spirit which results. The success of the process is enhanced by the communication of the attitude that "we are praying and seeking a pastor together." The roles of committee members and others in the church are obviously different in the process, but the role of all is important!

Listening sessions.—The committee may choose to meet with selected groups to ask certain questions and note responses. These groups may include deacons, Church Council, men's groups, women's groups, youth, children, senior adults, and even a group of attenders who have not yet joined.

Questions may vary from group to group, but they should always be open-ended. They may include such questions as:
- What are the nonnegotiables of what our new pastor must believe?
- What style of leadership should he have?
- What kind of preacher does he need to be?
- When he asks about our vision as a church, what should we tell him?
- What are your concerns as a group?
- When a prospective pastor asks us about our willingness to pray for him, follow him, and support him, what shall we tell him?
- If you could say one sentence to our prospective pastor, what would it be?

These questions may be adjusted into the vocabulary of the group (for example, in talking with children).

In conducting these listening sessions, the search committee should make them exactly that. Consider these suggestions.
- Resist the temptation to answer questions or reveal your personal views.
- Guide the process so that there is wide participation.
- Do not allow persons in the group to begin to discuss answers with one another.
- Do everything possible to create an openness and freedom where no one is intimidated or hesitant to have his or her say.
- Do not allow one or two to do all the talking. Occasionally a statement may need to be made such as, "Now let's hear from someone who has not yet spoken." This type of statement will broaden participation.

In listening sessions, one committee member should lead the discussion while another has the assignment of taking notes. The rest of the committee should listen carefully. Individual names will not be connected in the record with statements that are made, but what is said will be treated seriously. Immediately after the session, the committee should meet to listen to a reading of the notes of what was said and make them a part of their permanent record.

An alternate method for congregational input is to set aside a Sunday evening or Wednesday evening service, divide into groups of four to eight people for brainstorming. Then ask each group to share a report with the entire group. Be sure some of the groups are made up of children only and youth only. These groups can be insightful.

Chapter Eight

STUDYING YOUR CONGREGATION

By the time the search committee is ready to look at ministry candidates, it should know the kind of leader needed based on a thorough study of the congregation.[1]

REVIEW THE FUNCTIONAL HEALTH OF THE CHURCH

This exercise ought to be done by the search committee itself. A helpful book to use in guiding this process is *Kingdom Principles for Church Growth* by Gene Mims.[2]

This is a time for the committee to review the *purpose statement* or *vision statement* of the church. If the church does not have one, the committee ought to ask themselves, "In light of the Great Commission, why is our church here and what are we to do?" The committee can review and discuss how the church is doing in the five functions of the church: worship, evangelism, discipleship, ministry, and fellowship. The following questions can be answered:

- What are we doing well?
- What needs attention?
- What results are we seeing in spiritual growth, numerical growth, mission involvement, and ministry expansion?[3]
- How can a new pastor or staff minister make a difference in these areas?

This study ought not be time-consuming, but it will help the committee to use to the maximum the information gained from the previous exercises.

CONDUCT A MISCELLANEOUS REVIEW

Likely, by the time the committee has worked through the suggestions already mentioned, most issues have emerged. However, the committee may also want to ask and answer such questions as:

- Does the church have a debt that demands attention?
- Is a building program anticipated?
- Will the staff be supervised by the new minister? What are their ages? experience? uniquenesses?
- Does the church have unique ministries the new minister must lead or give attention to—television or radio, jail or prison, counseling, or other specialized ministries?
- Are there social or cultural expectations that go with the location or history of the church?
- Will educational or economic factors affect the expectations or demands on the new minister?
- Are there other similar questions?

ENVISION THE PASTOR OR STAFF MINISTER GOD WANTS YOU TO HAVE

The committee now ought to be able to develop a candidate profile. Some of the items listed will no doubt be flexible, but others will be nonnegotiable. Again, the clearer, simpler, and, perhaps, shorter the profile the better. The following outline will give you a place to start in developing a candidate profile. However, it ought definitely to be customized to meet the needs of the particular church. No two churches are identical. Among the things which you may want to include in the candidate profile are:

Salvation experience.—The candidate needs to be able to articulate a definite conversion and have experienced at least ____ years of consistent Christian growth since being saved.

Call to ministry.—The candidate must be able to articulate clearly a call to the gospel ministry, and this must be clearly recognized by others who know the candidate.

Educational background.—The candidate must have the following educational preparation: _____. (Note: This is a good time to decide if Bible college or seminary is required, expected, helpful, or not a factor. If education is a factor, then what degrees and what accreditation of the institutions are preferred? If other preparation may offset educational requirements, this should be noted as well.)

Ministerial experience.—The candidate needs to have ____ years of experience as a pastor (or particular staff ministry). This should include:

- Having served at least one church for a minimum of _____ years.
- Experience in a congregation with an attendance of at least _____.
- Indication of being a personal soul-winner with a strong baptismal history in the churches served.
- Experience in _____ (tailored to the immediate needs of the church, i.e. leading a building program, debt retirement, staff supervision, etc.)
- Demonstration of strong interpersonal relationship skills, strong work habits, and denominational loyalty.

Gifts and passions.—The candidate must possess call, character, and competences which are demonstrated through ministry skills in:

- *Communication.*—The candidate must possess strong pulpit skills (or similar skills relating to one's ministry area).
- *Leadership.*—The candidate's current church should demonstrate his ability to grasp a vision, articulate that vision, and enlist a following.
- *Administration.*—The candidate must possess basic organizational skills.
- *Ministry.*—The candidate must have a pastor's heart demonstrated by the care shown in his present church. The purpose of the profile is to establish minimum standards with which the committee can work. Once ratified, it should be changed only with the strong consensus of the committee. The profile should free the committee to take the prayerful support of the congregation, information gathered, and unique insight given them by the Holy Spirit and concentrate responsibly on the assignment given them.

---

[1] This chapter is adapted from Frank Lewis, *Team Builder* (Nashville: Convention Press, 1997), 133-5.
[2] Gene Mims, *Kingdom Principles for Church Growth* (Nashville: Convention Press, 1994).
[3] Ibid.

Chapter Nine

DEVELOPING A CHURCH AND COMMUNITY PROFILE

The prospective minister will want to know as many details as possible about the church and community he is being asked to consider. Many committees find that a good way to do this is to develop an extensive notebook into which much valuable information can be placed. Sections of it should be removable so they can be duplicated. Also, several copies should be made for the committee to use and to share with the most serious candidates. Due to its extensive nature, the committee will likely ask that a particular candidate return the notebook if he is no longer being considered. Keep final copies on file at the church for reference and possible future use. Among the items that might be included are these:

- A copy of the vision and purpose statements of the church.
- Any adopted goals and directions for the next three to five years which the church has formally adopted.
- A current copy of the church's constitution and bylaws.
- A copy of the latest associational annual.
- An up-to-date history of the church.—Churches can sectionalize their history by giving the names, pastoral dates, and a few paragraphs summarizing the major accomplishments of the church during each pastor's tenure. Reference may also be made to the age of the pastor when he came, his most positive gifts,

and where he served before and after his tenure with this church.

- The names of all paid staff members who have served the church.—If these ministers have made significant impacts on the church, apart from those that would reflect on the historical overview and the church's statistics, these should be noted.

- A statistical history of the church.—This can be done in a year-by-year style using statistics that are normally listed on the Annual Church Profile. The membership flow, baptismal record and other additions, average attendance in Sunday School and worship, financial receipts, and missions giving can provide real insights as to what was going on in the life of the church at any given time. Insights can often be gained by the candidate as he cross-references this chart with the pastoral information.

- The most up-to-date church directory.—Pictures of choirs, leadership groups, and even family and individual pictures can help the prospect get a glimpse of the personality of the church.

- A copy of the current budget, organizational chart, nominating committee, and committee on committees reports, and descriptions of unique ministries.— Also, generally accepted statements as to the needs and effectiveness of existing ministries and programs of all age groups within the church can be included.

- A year's supply of church newsletters, bulletins, and/or church calendar.— These can convey a great deal of information.

- Pictures of current or former buildings.—These depict the personality, ministry, and history of the church. Also, a discussion of the condition of current buildings and a projected building upgrade or expansion depict much about the church presently as well as its vision and direction.

- City or county maps and other information.—These can often be obtained from the chamber of commerce or tourism office.

- Current and projected demographics.—Some of this information can be obtained from the association, state convention, or North American Mission Board. Other information can be obtained from the library, county/city zoning and planning board, and the local school board.

- A profile of the person the church should call as their next pastor or staff minister as determined by the search committee.—The committee may or may not want to include this depending on a variety of factors. For example, if the profile is simply a working document for the committee, it probably ought not be public knowledge. Also, if the profile is subject to change, it might cause a good candidate who does not meet the letter of the profile to withdraw from consideration. On the other hand, if the profile has been adopted by the church, it certainly ought to be included in information shared with any serious candidate.

Chapter Ten

REVIEWING BIOGRAPHICAL PROFILES

Once the candidate profile has been developed and adopted by the committee, it is time to begin to review biographical profiles. If a set cutoff date has not been given to the church and to others for submitting biographical profiles, it should be done at this point. If any sources of biographical profiles have been written from which a response has not been received, now is a good time to write a final reminder.

Even before the closing date to receive profiles, begin preliminary review of those already received. The committee will discover that many of those already received can, in light of the profile, immediately be eliminated. Of those that fit the criteria or come close, no attempt should be made to rank them. They should simply be kept in an active file at least until the cutoff date for receiving additional profiles has arrived.

NARROWING THE GROUP OF PROFILES

For those who are definitely eliminated, who are aware that the committee has their material, the committee should send a gentle, positive letter thanking them for their interest, informing them that they are no longer under consideration, and freeing them to consider other ministry possibilities. The letter should not include any details as to why they are no longer under consideration. (A letter is suggested rather than a phone call since it can be worded more precisely without having to get into a discussion that might betray confidences of the committee.) If they or someone representing them were to call demanding to know why (and it does happen), the answer should be kind, straightforward, and truthful. Such an answer might be: "In light of our predetermined criteria based on the expectations of our church, we simply did not feel led of God to move in your direction. We wanted you to know this because of your deep involvement in your current ministry and other opportunities God may provide for you."

Often a minister may have difficulty staying as focused as he should on his current ministry if he knows he is being considered by another church. Also, ministers have missed the opportunity to be considered by a second search committee while they wait to hear from a preferred committee, when unbeknown to them they have already been eliminated from consideration by the first committee. Once eliminated, candidates would rather know.

When those who obviously do not fit your church's profile have been eliminated, do not be surprised or discouraged if most of the biographical profiles have been eliminated. This is one reason it is not a good idea for the committee to announce to the church, "We have received more than one hundred biographical profiles" (or some other large number). Reality is that you have not received information on nearly that many viable candidates. Also, such an announcement can cause some people to think pastors (or staff ministers) suitable for your church are in abundance. And it may give the false idea that all of those who would make excellent ministers for your church are eager to be considered by your committee. Many of them, if they indeed were to be contacted by your committee, would eliminate themselves because they are happy where they are or are more interested in another opportunity.

UNDERSTANDING BIOGRAPHICAL PROFILES

What your committee is trying to do is find the *one* that God wants to bring to your church. So it doesn't really matter how many biographical profiles the committee receives as long as the right one is in hand.

What about these biographical profiles? From where do they come? What is the preparer trying to accomplish? The committee will discover that these biographical profiles represent all kinds of persons.

Among the situations are:

Those who are "just checking."—A minister has been where he is for some time and is mostly happy in his present ministry. If God does not open other doors, he'll be satisfied to stay where he is for a number of additional years. Yet he has reached a point of being willing to consider other ministry options. In his prayer life, he is asking, "Is the time right for me to consider a move?" If the committee is interested in talking with him, he will talk. He'll pray about a move; and if he feels that God is in it, he'll consider your church.

Those who are "always in circulation."—A minister in this category has had a series of two-year ministries. He simply has a restless spirit. He may have had good short-term ministries and left the churches better than he found them. Or he may have a pattern of leaving churches in disarray. Yet others have the misfortune of serving a number of churches that no one could have served for long. Some who have had a series of short-term ministries, break the pattern, stay for a longer time, and have effective ministries. Such a pattern does not mean that this candidate ought to be automatically eliminated; however, it does mean that special caution is wise in investigating and interviewing before proceeding with a possible relationship.

Those who are "growing persons."—God has used them where they have served, but they have obvious gifts that exceed the possibilities of their present ministries. Perhaps the only things lacking are experience and maturity. For some of these individuals, their next move may result in a benchmark ministry. Age may be a factor here but not always. These candidates, to be considered, require that a committee look not just at their track records but also at their potential.

Those who are "not in the right place."—Some ministers, for whatever reason, are just not in the right place for their best abilities to show forth. This may simply be in the mind of the minister, or it may indeed be reality. How did this happen? A minister may have made a mistake in going to where he currently ministers. He may have definitely been led there at the time because God needed someone with his particular gifts at that particular place at that particular time, but in the long term it is not where God has in mind for him to be. Virtually every long-term minister can look back on one or more places where God led him to accomplish a particular thing that was needed in the short-term to help the church get back on track. This kind of call may have been a sacrificial call on the part of the minister, but this type of ministry will never show impressive statistical growth. This is a reminder that often a minister ought not to be evaluated on only his current place of service. What about his previous church and the one before that?

Those who are "ready for a new challenge."—This minister has a good track record, but he has simply reached a point where he may have led his current church as far as he can take it. God will lead someone else to follow him, build on his ministry, and lead this church further toward where God wants it to be. Thus, in his spirit he senses that it is time to communicate through various avenues open to him that it is time for him to consider a move.

Those who are "under pressure to move."—For these individuals, someone or a group of persons in his current place of service is trying to force him out. Maybe the situation has not reached that point, but some in the church are making it difficult for him to minister effectively. The time to make a move is drawing near. The problem may be of his own creation, or it may be beyond his control. Sometimes this kind of situation causes a good pastor or staff minister to be available; but, as always, investigation is the key.

Those who are "open."—They may have been asked if their name could be given to your committee. They are not really sure why, but it seemed like the thing to do. Maybe something about your church aroused an interest—the church's location, its potential, its reputation, its need, or maybe a reason that would be hard even to articulate. Something has aroused an interest. Sometimes the Holy Spirit's work is difficult to explain.

Those who are "trying to get back in."—Some ministers, because they were forced out of a place of service, became disillusioned; or they succumbed to a mistake or sin and have been out of vocational ministry for a while. Now because that call has not died, they are seeking to start over. Many of these bring baggage, but some bring experience that will prove invaluable. Are these viable candidates? Some absolutely are. For many, what happened in the past was not their fault. With others the mistake was clearly theirs, but they have dealt with it before God in forgiveness and victory. With still others, perhaps they are viable candidates but should be considered carefully. Yet others have disqualified themselves from consideration by your search committee. Each one must be dealt with individually in light of the individual and the convictions, personality, and needs of the individual congregation.

Those who are "trying to get started."—The basic problem with these persons is a lack of experience. Their potential may be obvious, or it may be well hidden. Someone needs to help this minister get started. If this is indeed God's will for your church at this time, you will be helping a minister get started; and your church will be blessed in the process. Certainly, many situations simply cannot be a beginning place for a young or inexperienced minister, but every minister has to have that first experience.

The above list of ministers is not exhaustive. There are overlaps, and they are not listed in any order of preference, but these categories will help a search committee understand that biographical sketches represent real ministers who bring real-life backgrounds. Some of these backgrounds are good, and some are not so good. Others are not necessarily one or the other; they are simply realities. The "leadership path" found in the book *Kingdom Leadership* by Michael Miller will prove helpful as the committee prayerfully evaluates the biographical profiles which it has and will receive.[1]

---

[1] Michael Miller, *Kingdom Leadership: A Call to Christ-centered Leadership* (Nashville: Convention Press, 1996).

Chapter Eleven

FINDING THE WILL OF GOD

Someone has rightly said, "To know the will of God is life's greatest knowledge, and to do the will of God is life's greatest achievement." This truth certainly applies to the work of a search committee!

The search committee has reached the cutoff time for receiving biographical profiles. It has eliminated a number of profiles of those who obviously did not meet the criteria of the profile parameters developed by the committee. A number of biographical profiles remain before the committee; these are potential candidates. How does the committee move toward finding the will of God? It is not a simple process. The committee is faced with answering the question: How can we know and do the will of God?

I suggest that the committee as a group take the time to read and study Romans 12:1-6. In this passage Paul discussed the "good, and acceptable, and perfect, will of God" (KJV). He was not talking about the permissive will of God or the ultimate will of God, but he was talking about God's best plan for us in the decisions we face. The context assumes two important factors—a surrendered life (v. 1) and a willingness to do God's will within the context of the body of Christ, the church (v. 4).

In other words, we must be a surrendered people willing to do that which is best for the welfare of the kingdom, the body of Christ, the church. Against this backdrop, the committee can make great progress in dealing with individual profiles alongside the church's profile by asking these questions:

• Is it sensible?
• Is it spiritual?
• Is it scriptural?

Is It Sensible?

Notice the number of times in verses 2-3 that the passage uses the words "*mind*" and "*think*." In application to this process, the committee should ask, "In light of what we know about God, what we know about our church, and what we know about this candidate, does it make sense that he could be the person God wants to bring to our church at this time?" We are to use our brains! Our thinking is to be that of a "renewed," "transformed" or renovated mind. This means a thinking that is different from the secular or business model. It means looking at the gifts of the individual involved (vv. 3,6) and the needs of the church as best the committee can ascertain them. Again ask, "Does it make sense that this person may be the one God wants at our church at this time?"

Is It Spiritual?

Look at verses 1-2 again. As we surrender to God's will, the Holy Spirit has a way of impressing on our "renewed mind" the thought He wants us to have. This means that God may simply give within us a feeling of "oughtness." Often committee members make statements like: "_____'s biographical material just seems to keep coming back to the top for me." "At this point, I feel impressed that we ought to look further at _____." Sometimes specifics can be pointed to as being the hook the Holy Spirit seems to have used to grab someone's attention. It may be something in the candidate's background, a particular word used in his testimony, where the person appears to be on the "leadership path," or some other factor. It may be a matter of having the experience of looking in the direction God is looking (see Ps. 32:8).

Because God seems to be causing the committee to look at a particular person, does this mean the committee can be certain this candidate is the one? Not necessarily. God has a way of working step-by-step to reveal His will. My third pastorate came as a result of a search committee being confident that a particular pastor was the one to whom God was leading them. Were they right in going in that direction? Yes. Was he the one God wanted to be their pastor? No. Each time the committee approached this pastor, his response was no. Then each time he recommend someone else. After this happened a number of times, the committee decided to follow his recommendation and look at the person whose profile they did not even have. That recommendation turned out to be the one that God was directing the committee toward all along.

Is It Scriptural?

This ought to go without saying, but it needs to be said again anyway. Is there anything in the candidate's life that morally or spiritually does not line up with Scripture, thus eliminating him from the committee's consideration? Does he hold doctrinal views that do not stand the test of Scripture? How does his ministry measure up to the clear commands of such passages as the Great Commandments and the Great Commission?

These three questions can be used as guidelines to focus the evaluation of each profile to decide whether it ought to be kept active and/or in what order it ought to be ranked by the committee.

Chapter Twelve

RANKING THE FINAL GROUP OF CANDIDATES

Using the criteria in the last chapter (or some similar biblical approach) and the candidate profile parameters the committee has developed, it is now time to narrow the list and to rank candidates in priority order.

First, the number of biographical profiles under consideration needs to be reduced to a small number. A suggested ideal is five. How can this be done? The ways are numerous. A couple of sample methods are suggested:

One week prior to a committee meeting designated for reducing and ranking the profiles under consideration, each committee member is asked to take all of the profiles under consideration for a time of prayer and evaluation. The assignment is to assign each profile to one of three categories—excellent, good, or average.

If the search committee has seven members, collect those which receive at least four excellent ratings. If the committee has five members, group those with three excellents. Once these profiles have been placed in a group, make sure every member of the committee has in hand a copy of each of these and only these. Have each committee member pray and meditate over them. Then review the profiles to rank them from one through the number of profiles (1 for the first choice, 2 for the second choice, etc.) This should not be rushed. When this has been done, the numbers on each candidate should be added with the lowest total being the highest rank. At this point the top five (can be expanded to six or seven, if that appears to be feasible) should become the active group which will be dealt with one at a time.

A second method is to divide the committee into teams of two (alternates can be added to even up teams). Each team then reviews each active profile to determine a top 10 with the highest ranked candidate being given a 10, second highest a 9, etc. Then the total committee reviews every candidate. For those who were ranked by any of the teams in the top 10, that number is written by the candidate's name. When the number is added up, the candidate with the highest number is rated first, the second highest rated second, until a top five or seven is determined.

The committee should begin to deal with the candidates one at a time, beginning with the highest candidate. That candidate should be the only one being actively dealt with until a conclusion to call, eliminate, or, in some cases, rerank the profile.

With any method, as a top five or seven is being determined, committee members should feel free to discuss among themselves why they ranked candidates as they did. On occasion, this will cause someone to rerank the candidates. If a consensus is difficult or impossible to reach, more time may be needed. The committee may need to retreat to an early point in the process and move through the steps again. It may also mean that more candidates are needed. If that is the case, call previous or additional sources. This, also, may be a time to slow down and see if other biographical profiles are received.

Further discussion among the committee as to strengths and weaknesses, qualities or characteristics someone has detected, the reputation of recommenders, and other matters brought out in the open may be helpful. If no clear pattern develops, there is no need to panic. God is sovereignly in control of the entire process, and His timing will be perfect.

At this point the committee should make a decision about profiles they will continue to receive. If the committee feels good about the candidates under consideration, any new recommendations should be held by the recorder (or other designated person) until and if a time comes when the whole process is reopened. This may happen if the process bogs down with the top two or three candidates.

Should the committee ever deal with more than one candidate at a time? Early in the process more than one candidate may be in the picture. For example, if three of the candidates obviously are ranked close and rise above the others, the committee may determine that the first choice will be more actively pursued while at the same time preliminary reference checks on the other two may be done. The danger in this is the potential of dividing the committee, especially if different persons are checking references on different candidates. The advantage is that, if the top choice turns out not to be the Lord's man for your church, the committee can more quickly move to candidate number two and so on until the process has been completed.

Chapter Thirteen

FOCUSING ON ONE SERIOUS CANDIDATE

Now that the committee has focused on one primary candidate with a couple of back-up possibilities, what happens next? A lot of factors affect how the committee ought to proceed. There is no right or wrong way as long as the committee is ethical in all proceedings and honest with all candidates. The golden rule certainly applies here. As committee members put themselves in the position of each candidate under consideration, they will indeed treat him as they themselves would want to be treated.

A PREFERRED METHOD

The committee should begin by telephoning the prospect to determine whether he wishes to be considered at this time. Do not be discouraged if he is dealing with another committee and declines for now to be considered by your committee. If such is the case, do not promise to call back later but make a note as to when it might be appropriate. Do not confuse the issue for him by expressing too high a level of interest. (At this point it is impossible to know how interested the committee would actually be if he were available to negotiate.) As you need to deal with one candidate at a time, he needs to deal with one committee at a time.

If the candidate indicates an openness to be considered, permission should be obtained to hear the candidate preach and to check the references he has given. If there are references which should not be called in this first round, such as members of his current church, this should be noted in the discussion. Usually the candidate has no objections to references being checked. If the candidate objects, this could be cause enough for the committee to look for someone else.

If the search committee is for a pastor, most churches will view preaching as important. A time should be determined when the pastor will be in the pulpit preaching a "normal" sermon. Some committees fear that letting the candidate know they are coming will cause him to preach a "sugar stick." However, it doesn't take long to know whether the candidate is preaching to the congregation or to the committee.

This first visit should be seen as information gathering. An interview is not scheduled yet. This visit provides an opportunity to listen, observe, and participate in worship. Listening to a candidate preach will give more insights into his abilities and gifts than any interview will. While interpersonal skills are extremely important, most people still come to church to hear a sermon.

Following the visit, the committee should meet to discuss their observations. Both the sermon's content and delivery should be discussed. In addition, how did the preacher relate to other staff members and interact with his people? Of the church, how were members of the committee welcomed? Would committee members attend this church again if they lived in the community? Did the people say anything to a committee member about their pastor? What strengths and weaknesses of the church were observed during the visit? Why should these questions be discussed? A church will in many ways reflect the personality of its pastor-leader. If committee members noted anything unusual, these might be noted for discussion with the candidate later.

At this point one of three things ought to happen.

1. The committee will be interested in pursuing this candidate.

2. The committee is ready to eliminate him from further consideration.

3. The committee likes some things but were not as impressed about other things. As a result, the committee as a whole is just not sure.

The decision of what happens next depends on which of these three conclusions is reached. If the third conclusion above has been reached, the chairperson should telephone with an expression of appreciation for the visit and inform the candidate that the committee would like to leave the possibilities open and a statement that the committee would like to hear a couple of other persons. His response may be that after prayerful consideration he suggests the committee move on to someone else, or he may say that he will be open to further discussions in the future.

Of course, if the second conclusion is reached, the candidate should receive a call from the chairperson expressing appreciation for the visit with positive, honest affirmations of the experience but that the committee feels led to pursue other directions. It cannot be overemphasized that this call ought to be handled with utmost dignity, affirmation, and love. The committee is dealing with the ministry of a man of God.

Assuming both the committee and the pastor are interested in proceeding further, a second meeting should be arranged. This visit should include the pastor's spouse and family. Perhaps a meal together at a restaurant a few miles from the church would be an excellent opportunity for getting acquainted. This likely will allow the candidate to drive through the church's community, see the building, and observe the setting.

In this second meeting the candidate should be given the material prepared in the profile of the church and community. Important doctrinal issues, style of leadership, and philosophy of ministry ought to be discussed. If there are unusual matters in the life of the church of which the candidate ought to be aware (most committees instinctively know what these are), this is a good time to bring them out in the open. He should be asked if he possesses any unusual beliefs or practices of which the committee should be aware. (He will know what these are, as well). Remember that this is a 50-50 interview. Half of it belongs to the candidate; half of it belongs to the committee. Both parties have the right and responsibility to learn as much about each other as possible. For this visit, as well as on other occasions, when expenses are incurred by prospective candidates, your church should reimburse travel and other expenses incurred by the minister.

Following this exploratory visit, both parties need information about each other; and they need time. By the time the meeting is over, the candidate should have in hand, in addition to detailed information about the church and community, details regarding salary, benefits, expectations, and responsibilities. If not included in other material, he should be provided information about all staff persons. Be sure that an area map, information about schools, a realtor's brochure, and a recent newspaper are given as well.

The committee may ask for permission to hear the pastor preach again in person and/or on tape (audio or video) for three or four recent, consecutive Sundays. Your chairman may ask for permission to check with references beyond those given by the candidate, with the assurance that none of his current members will be called without his permission.

Forms should be signed by the candidate allowing the church to check criminal and financial histories. (These are musts.) It may be simpler for the candidate to have a certified credit check prepared through a credit bureau where he lives, but the committee should have the criminal check done through a law enforcement office. These will likely be routine and inconsequential; but, if there is a problem, the committee needs to know now.

Both parties now need time and permission to investigate each other. Permission should be granted for the candidate and the chairman to be in continual contact. Questions will arise from both parties, many of which can be answered with a phone call.

ALTERNATE METHODS

If the first method for arriving at one serious candidate is not well suited for the committee, it may want to consider other possibilities. Usually these involve doing preliminary investigation on three to five candidates before narrowing the focus to one. If this is the approach to be taken, the chairperson (or others) may call all candidates to determine whether they are interested in being considered. If there is mutual interest, some or all of the following can be done.

Hear all candidates preach.—This preliminary visit need not be announced. However, before traveling a great distance, the committee may want to ensure that the candidate will in the pulpit on that particular Sunday. Every attempt should be made to be as inconspicuous as possible. The committee may want to separate or to be seated two by two. They should not fill out visitors cards. Greet fellow worshipers, but attract as little attention as possible. Take only mental notes; simply listen and observe. As the committee travels back home, observations should be discussed and recorded. As much as possible, all candidates should be heard and observed in similar settings.

Call potential candidates, asking for three or four sermon tapes.—If this is done, obviously video is better, and consecutive sermons are preferred. Although this approach may be economically and logistically more feasible than personal visits, many things can never be captured on videotape. Also, some good candidates may not have tapes available. Remember, nonprofessional recordings can give a less-than-accurate impression of the pastor and his sermons.

Ask all candidates to respond in writing to a series of questions.—These can include a statement regarding his conversion experience, call to ministry, basic beliefs, philosophy of ministry, description of preaching style, beliefs about worship, view of Sunday School, philosophy of deacon ministry, assessment of strengths and weaknesses, a list of accomplishments, and/or a statement as to why he is open to a move. I recommend that the questionnaire be preceded by a phone call. If it is simply received in the mail with a cover letter, some of the best candidates will not take the time to complete the form. They have received similar requests before and will assume that they are 1 of 25 or more who are being considered. Also, it is a one-sided situation when a committee is asking them to respond when they have little or no information about the church. This process is time-consuming for a busy minister. If he is to respond to such an inquiry, he wants to know enough to decide whether he has an interest in the church.

Interview each candidate either in person or by a conference call.—The advantage is that each candidate can be asked the same questions. Responses can either be recorded through notes or on audiotape. The disadvantage is that it is usually awkward for both the committee and the candidate.

If this second approach is taken, the lead candidates should then be dealt with in much the same fashion as discussed under the first approach. At this point, the committee should deal with one candidate at a time.

In calling a staff minister the same processes may be followed with the differences being that the pastor should be deeply involved in the process. He, along with the chairman, should make the calls and set up visits. And, of course, preaching would likely not be a part of the evaluation.

Chapter Fourteen

INVESTIGATING EACH OTHER

Beyond the list of references given by the candidate and official police and financial checks, where does a committee go to learn more about a candidate? Among those who should know a minister in any community are funeral directors, hospital personnel, bankers, grocers, druggists, automobile dealers, fellow pastors (different denominations are often helpful), former pastors, and former staff ministers of the church he serves, and denominational leaders. Often some members of the search committee will have occupational relationships with persons in similar occupations in the community where the minister serves. (Be aware that some of the persons called may be members of the church he serves.) Also, calls ought to be made to leadership persons in all of the churches where the minister has previously served. These persons ought to be extremely objective in their evaluations. Remember, however, that no one is liked by everybody (see Luke 6:26). A reference may tell you as much about the one giving the reference as it does the candidate, so do not let one negative reference color your opinion too strongly.

With references, patterns may be noted. To some, the probing of references may seem extreme, but it is better to know both negatives and positives before the partnership is established than to discover severe problems later.

How does an interested candidate investigate a church? The methods are similar to those above. The same types of people may be called. Plus, he may wish to call the current interim pastor, former pastors, former members (names should be obtained from the chairperson), and current staff members (with permission of the committee).

Sample questions for use by the committee and the candidate can be found in the *Pastor and Staff Search Committee Kit.*

Chapter Fifteen

DEALING WITH ONE CANDIDATE AT A TIME

Now that the committee has obtained detailed, confidential, and personal information about their best candidate, what should be their next step? If the committee, after serious and often lengthy prayer sessions seeking the will of God, in light of the information obtained, feels led of the Holy Spirit to proceed further with a particular candidate, progress is being made. The candidate should then be contacted to see if he feels the same. If so, an additional meeting should be set up for deep discussion and prayer. This should probably be at the committee's church and may involve staff, if they have not previously been involved. The staff probably should not be in on all detailed discussions but should be present as appropriate. Staff ministers or committee members may serve as hosts for church building tours and community tours.

What if, before or after this meeting, the committee or the candidate does not feel good about continuing the process? If it is a matter of time, reasonable time should be granted to the hesitant party. However, if it is just not a good match, the party which has reached this conclusion should candidly and lovingly say so (see Eph. 4:15). At this point the rejected party has a right to know why.

If and when discussion ends with a particular candidate, the committee should simply go to the next candidate and profile and begin the process at the appropriate point with the next candidate. If not only the top candidate but also other top candidates do not seem to be the right match (or maybe one or more has withdrawn), this may be a good time to revert back to a review of all candidates not eliminated previously. Also, this may be an appropriate time to bring new biographical profiles into the mix. Many churches have found the right candidate through a second review or a late-arriving group of profiles. Do not be discouraged; constantly seek God's will. He is guiding the process. How many times can a committee revert back to a previous point in the process? As often as necessary to find the one candidate God has in mind.

When one candidate has become the extended focus of the committee, and there is strong mutual interest, the matter becomes more and more serious. With this one candidate the committee and he are becoming more and more confident of God's leadership in the direction of a ministry partnership. It is now time to conduct an intense, earnest, candid, probing interview.

Chapter Sixteen

PREPARING TO PRESENT THE CANDIDATE TO THE CHURCH

In this last formal interview before the candidate is brought before the church for consideration, every matter that has not been considered must be addressed; every matter of significance that has been discussed needs to be reviewed.

The candidate should be asked to bring to the meeting a list of questions he would like to have answered, his personal and church calendar, and a tentative pastor (or staff minister) and church agreement. This will help the committee and the candidate to:

Clarify remaining questions and concerns.—The candidate will want to make sure his understanding is clear and accurate regarding:

• The congregation's expectations of him and his wife.
• The congregation's understanding of and commitment to its mission.
• Whether the church is inward or outward looking.
• Why he is of particular interest to them as their potential pastor.
• The most recent significant problems in the life of the congregation and their current status. (All churches have them. What are they for this congregation?)
• Recent victories the church has experienced and the significance they have for the future.
• The greatest needs in the church.

- The kinds of things the last pastor did well and those he did not do as well as needed by this church.
- Building plans or ministry changes needed to accomplish what God has in mind for the church.[1]

The committee will want to make sure their understanding is clear regarding:
- Any doctrinal concerns that have come to light.
- Any questions about any items uncovered by their investigations.
- How the minister feels about the challenges and expectations of the church
- The salary package, provisions, and benefits.
- The relocation arrangements.
- The time frame required to make the transition.[2]

Be open with the prospect about church problems.—The candidate needs to be informed of any recent or deep-seated problems within the church that might affect his decision to accept or reject an invitation to lead your church. Do not assume that a problem is too insignificant to be discussed. The candidate, if he feels God wants him to lead your church, will accept your invitation regardless of problems you reveal.

But he and you are much more likely to have a happy experience together if he is not shocked and disappointed to find after becoming your pastor that there were problems about which he should have been told and was not. Openness and honesty are always the best policies.

Be open, official, and generous in financial provisions.—Be sure that all financial matters are thoroughly discussed and given to the candidate in written form.

The committee may need to meet with the finance committee regarding salary. Any changes need to be approved by the church. In establishing a salary package for the pastor or staff minister, take the time to read 1 Timothy 5:17-18.

The church needs to understand that basic benefit packages including retirement, insurance, convention, travel, and similar expenses which enable the minister to serve your church should not be considered as part of his salary. For most employed persons these items are consider a part of the employee's provisions required for him to do the job. In a corresponding way, the minister's salary package should include salary and housing allowance. The other items certainly should be provided but not stated as part of the minister's salary.

In deciding the minister's salary, factors such as education and experience should be considered. Also, many congregations are in a position to assist with special family needs he may have. In short, the salary and housing package should be as generous as the congregation can provide. Also, it must be clearly communicated to the candidate the procedure of the church for salary review and when increases can be expected. God will bless the congregation that is faithful in providing for the ministers He gives to the church.

Many state conventions, through the church relations department, can provide a study of pastor and staff salaries. This will allow the committee to evaluate what other churches of similar size and budget provide for pastor with similar experience and education. This can be a valuable tool but should never be used in an effort to get by with paying a lesser salary than what the church can reasonably provide.

Discuss the procedure.—This meeting should end with both the committee and the candidate being clear as to what is to happen next. If the committee issues an invitation to preach, when can the candidate expect that invitation to be officially given? If such an invitation is extended by the committee, when can they expect the candidate to accept or decline the invitation? Is additional time needed by one or both before moving on with the decision? If so, it is better to be cautious than to have second thoughts later. Are additional meetings or further information needed? If so, when and what? If an answer is needed from one or both parties, when can that answer be expected? If both parties still feel good about proceeding, two tasks need to be accomplished.

Develop a tentative timetable.—Review the church's constitution and bylaws to see how this is to be done. A timetable which meets and exceeds the requirements should be mutually agreed upon. What time commitments and responsibilities are being asked of the candidate? What material does he need to supply to the committee (picture, biographical sketch, etc)? When and of what nature will public announcements regarding the visit be made (again, be careful to meet bylaws requirements)? What arrangements will the committee make in preparation for the weekend. Where will he and his family stay? What meetings will the committee set up? How many times is he to preach? When will the vote be taken? What percentage of vote is required for selection? Is this suitable to the candidate, or would he or the committee expect a higher percentage? If the vote is positive, when can an answer be expected from the candidate?

Even if all the above questions cannot be answered, preliminary discussion will help. This discussion will again remind all who are involved just how serious the decision is that they are about to make. It must be bathed in prayer!

Develop a pastor (or staff minister) and church agreement.—This document should be the beginning point of a minister's relationship with a church. It can be presented to the church for adoption at the same time as the salary and benefits package (as discussed previously) or specified on certain schedules immediately before the candidate's visit on Sunday (as discussed later). This document should be negotiated by the committee bringing their proposal to the meeting and the minister bringing his proposal.

This should not be a standardized document which the committee simply presents to the candidate. It ought to be negotiated and customized to the needs and desires of the candidate. For example, preaching a certain number of revivals may be important to one candidate. Another may have a keen interest in continuing education provisions. Still another may have reached a certain vacation level in his present ministry, and it would be unfair to ask him to forfeit that in order to serve your church. Therefore, customization is a reasonable approach.

The minister-church agreement ought to document matters relating to salary and benefits; vacation, days off, revivals, and other times away from the church ministries; convention attendance; continuing education; moving provisions; and other matters. This is a beginning document and may be changed at any time by mutual agreement of the church and the minister. Most obviously, the salary ought to be adjusted annually at budget adoption. Other matters can be changed as agreed to by parties involved. (See the sections regarding housing and moving expenses.)

This document is not a contract. Its primary purpose it to help ensure that once the minister has accepted the church's invitation the promises made to him have been documented. The search committee will not remain active; and, even if it did, the passing of time has a way of dimming the recollection of what was promised the minister in the process of his being called to the church.

During these negotiations is a good time for the committee and the candidate to discuss the subject of minister-church conflict. What will the church do in the future if a conflict arises with the minister as to leadership style, a disagreement over church direction, or even perceptions of misconduct? On the other hand, what is the pastor or staff minister to do if he feels mistreated by the church or individuals within the congregation? No one enjoys dealing with those matters or bringing up the potential of their occurrence. Yet they do occur—frequently!

Why not set up a procedure now rather than when it is too late. If they are never needed, wonderful! But if they are, all will be grateful that the minister and search committee had the foresight to broach the subject. Who brings the subject up? Either the committee or the candidate can open this line of talk. This does not necessarily indicate a past problem for either but wisdom and openness. Indeed, the very discussion of the subject will likely lead the candidate and the committee to further openness and bonding. (A sample document can be found in the *Pastor and Staff Search Committee Kit.*)

---

[1] Adapted from Paul Nix, "On Seeing and Being Seen," *Church Administration*, July 1997, 24-8.
[2] Ibid.

Chapter Seventeen

PREPARING A WEEKEND VISIT IN VIEW OF A CALL

Any scheduling of a visit of the minister to the church in view of a call should, to this point, be tentative. The committee should meet with no one else present (other than alternates) to come to a final conclusion regarding an official invitation to the candidate. Each member should feel free to express his or her feelings. If the committee is not unanimous about inviting him to your church, an invitation should not be extended. Neither should the prospect be pressured to make such a visit unless he is entirely positive. If either the candidate or the committee needs a reasonable amount of additional time before making a decision, that time should be granted. Preaching does not mean that it is a "done deal," but it does mean that both the committee and the candidate are confident that God is leading in that direction.

When the committee has its final vote, if one person's vote is negative, he or she should not be pressured to change his or her vote. God may be using this method to guide the committee toward finding His perfect will in the search process. Believing that He is sovereignly guiding the search, no one on the committee should become disappointed or frustrated over temporary delays. In time, God's plan will become evident to each member of the committee.

If a unanimous invitation cannot be extended to the candidate, he ought to be told. I believe this should be done by telephone. Every effort should be made to affirm the candidate's person and ministry; yet he needs to be informed as soon as possible. The committee should then "take a deep breath," regroup, and begin again at the appropriate place in the process.

If the candidate is unsure, a reasonable amount of additional time should be set aside for him to pray and consider. His sincere effort to find the will of God should be respected. If the candidate turns the committee down, even at this point, he and the committee should feel that this is the will of God. Certainly, the committee would want to call him as pastor or staff minister only if he feels that it is the will of God.

Assuming both the committee and the candidate are ready for a visit in view of a call, again the committee should follow the church's constitution and bylaws to the letter. No shortcuts should be taken—even if some of the stipulations seem inappropriate. This is not the time to try to change the procedure and risk negative votes against the candidate because of some perceived or actual bylaw violation. As long as these fall within the parameters of the constitution and bylaws, the following suggestions are helpful:

Remember that the church is as much on trial as the candidate.—At this point, the committee and the church likely assume, if the vote is good, the minister will accept the church's invitation. However, remember that the prospect has never actually met church members. He only knows the congregation through what he has been told by the committee. The dynamics of the group meetings, the open forum, and the preaching experience may differ from what was anticipated. In my 30-year pastoral ministry, I have preached six trial sermons and been called all six times; but I accepted only four of these invitations. The two that were declined were extremely strong votes (actually stronger than one of those accepted). Yet, in the struggle to find the will of God, in neither of these did the clearance come from God to say yes. Both churches were and are great churches. If this happens, the committee and the church must accept this as another way God is delaying the process until the time is perfect for Him to lead the committee to exactly the right person.

Separate any changes that need to be made to the salary and benefit package from the call vote.—Ideally, if financial adjustments need to be made or other sensitive matters decided, they should be dealt with in the church's regular business meeting before the announcement of the name and date of a trial sermon. If it is of such nature that it would be wise for the church to receive advance notice, a Sunday announcement immediately before the business meeting might be: "Wednesday your search committee will present to the church for action an item necessary in preparation for the calling of a new pastor (or staff minister)." Share it with all appropriate groups before the business meeting. Then present it in an open, informative way, deal with questions, and ask for a positive vote. This vote may be a strong indicator to the candidate as to whether the church is ready to issue him a call. Therefore, he should receive an accurate report from the business session—not only the action taken but also the spirit of the meeting.

Give the church at least two week's notice in preparation for the candidate's visit.—In some cases because of the candidate's present ministry, his name might be withheld until closer to the date of the actual visit. Nevertheless much about the candidate can be shared without giving his name. Use every appropriate means to communicate details about the candidate and his visit.

Invite the candidate to spend as much time as possible in the community in connection with the visit.—He and his family may be able to come early, allowing them time to become familiar with the area before the pressure of the meetings. This may help him to be more relaxed and, at the same time, create a more positive excitement for him and his family about their prospective new home. Also, perhaps they can have the option of staying a few extra days beyond the vote. If the call is good and he is ready to accept, this time can be spent locating housing or dealing with other matters related to the move. Remember, the church should pay all expenses, even paying for the minister's supply in the church he currently serves.

Develop a schedule which allows for maximum interaction with the congregation.—This may mean a Friday evening or a Saturday morning visit with the deacons and/or Church Council. It also may be good to schedule Saturday afternoon meetings with various age groups of the church. Saturday evening may be a good time for an open forum with the entire church invited. This is a good time for the candidate to share his salvation testimony, call to ministry, Christian pilgrimage, and philosophy of ministry. The congregation then should be allowed to ask questions and make comments. These should be dealt with in candor and Christian grace. Often the congregation is as interested in how the candidate deals with questions as with the actual answers.

The candidate and the committee may feel that these meetings involve the same people, the same testimonies, and the same concerns. This may indeed be true; but every time the candidate and the people are together, bonding is likely to occur. Too much exposure is far better than too little. After all, it is anticipated that this partnership will last for many years into the future.

Allow plenty of preaching time on Sunday morning.—Introduction of the candidate to the congregation should be presented in a positive fashion as the unanimous recommendation of the search committee. This will take time and should be planned. Indeed, plan the service so that he will have a little more time than the preacher might ordinarily have. More time will help him to relax and be himself rather than feel rushed.

Take the vote by secret ballot.—Most candidates would like to know the actual convictions of the congregation relating to a call. A voice vote or standing vote will make it less likely that all of the people will express their true feelings.

Many churches are finding that Sunday morning immediately after the sermon is a good time to vote. Most of the time this can be accommodated by announcing the time of the vote at the same time as announcing the visit of the candidate.

If the search committee is in relationship to a staff minister, much of the same procedure can be followed with the candidate meeting with appropriate groups, being introduced to the congregation on Sunday morning, participating in the morning activities in an appropriate fashion, and sharing a testimony in the evening service. The vote can be taken after the service on Sunday evening.

Other congregations believe that, with either a prospective pastor or a staff minister, the entire visit on Sunday should be spent getting acquainted with each other. The vote would be taken the following Sunday morning. In this approach, the prospective pastor would preach morning and evening. The primary disadvantage of this approach is a long week of waiting for everyone involved. Advantages include that of allowing the congregation to have more opportunities to observe the candidate and of allowing him to know even more about the congregation.

With this timetable, the Wednesday night following the visit on Sunday can be used as an opportunity to ratify the pastor (or staff minister) and church agreement. This document should have been developed and agreed on by the prospect and the committee before the candidate agreed to visit the church; but if it has not already been ratified by the church, it should be ratified before the vote to call. Also, if there is any reason to discuss any aspect of the call before it is extended, all discussion should be done during this Wednesday night service. That way Sunday morning's vote will be on issuing the call only. (Note: If this is not a regular business meeting night, it should be properly announced. The best way is at least two weeks before the visit Sunday to include the information in the worship bulletin, the church newsletter, and announcement times.[1]

The motion to call should be clear.—In the called business session announced for the purpose of conducting the one item of business—the extending of a call to a pastor or staff minister—a nondebatable motion should be made by the search committee chairman or some other person representing the search committee. Often it is best for the motion to be printed in the worship bulletin. The maker of the motion should read it, calling attention to it in written form, and move the action included in the motion. It may read something like this: "On behalf of the search committee, I move that Reverend (Doctor, Brother, or Mr.) _____ be called as our pastor (or _____ minister). This call is based on salary and benefits approved by our church in business session on _____(date) and the minister-church agreement approved on _____(date)." (If there is no change from the church budget, the motion should so note.)

If either the salary and benefit package or the minister-church agreement must be approved as a part of the call, this should be included in the motion. In any case, the motion should be kept as short and clear as possible. Once the motion is made, (It technically does not require a second since it is coming from a committee.) the vote should be taken immediately without discussion.

The votes should be counted immediately.—The moderator will normally appoint a counting committee whose chairperson will certify the numbers of votes and report in writing to the search committee's chairperson or representative. Also he will likely tell the church when and how the results of the vote will be announced to the congregation. Usually he will instruct the persons involved in the count, the search committee, and the church that the results are to be kept confidential until the entire church can know the results at the same time.

If the vote is taken at the close of a worship service, the results should be announced in the next worship service as well as the next publication of the church newsletter. If the vote is taken on Sunday evening, the church may want to continue the service until the vote result can be announced. This is emphasized to underscore the fact that the call is a decision of the entire congregation, and the whole church is to participate in the results.

The candidate is notified of the church's decision.—The chairman should give a report to the candidate immediately after the vote. If the chairman were to delay for any reason in sharing the results with the candidate, the latter likely will imagine all sorts of scenarios. If the vote is positive, anxiety can be removed and the excitement of the anticipated new partnership can be enhanced by a timely call. On the other hand, if the vote is sufficient to make the call official but not as strong as hoped, the candidate may need additional time to decide whether to accept or refuse the call. If the vote call does not meet the required percentage designated in the constitution and bylaws or predetermined agreement of the committee and/or candidate, the sooner this is reported to the candidate the better.

Even if the call is unanimous, or nearly so, the candidate may need time before giving an answer. Likely, even if he knows what his decision will be, out of respect for his present ministry, he will not want the calling church to announce his acceptance before he has had opportunity to resign from his current church. This should be respected by the minister's new church. Again, the golden rule should apply here.

The church is then notified of the candidate's decision.—As soon as possible within the guidelines discussed above, the church should be made aware of the exact vote on the candidate; and when permission has been granted by the candidate, his decision should be announced. If he has accepted the church's invitation, it is a time for celebration and prayerful dedication. This may be a time for applause, singing the doxology, calling the church to the altar for a season of prayer, or all of these. The arrival of new pastor is the inauguration of a new era. The coming of a new staff minister may take the church to a new level in its kingdom impact. This time is significant!

A failed call must be accepted and addressed.—What if the church does not issue a call? What if the call is weak, and the candidate declines? What if the call is strong and the anticipation high, yet the candidate declines? In any of these cases, the committee can expect obvious disappointment and emotional damage. Someone in the process inevitably feels rejected.

If a candidate is not issued a call, a closure visit (usually by phone) should be conducted. The committee should meet before the call to prepare an outline of what to communicate. The committee and the candidate have been in negotiation for some time. Friendships have been established. The disappointment is likely mutual. Thus, the closure call should be a time to express those disappointments, affirm each other, and speak the truth in love.

Were mistakes made by the candidate? He should know of these, for the sake of his learning, for he will deal with other churches. Did the committee make serious mistakes in presenting him to the church? These should be acknowledged and forgiveness sought. Was the timing bad or conditions in the church such that a good call would not have been possible for anyone? Talk frankly about these, but do not become hypercritical of your church. It is your church, and it is God's church. On rare occasions, a congregation may be led to reconsider a candidate, but this is rarely a good idea. The factors that prevented a good call the first time will likely be exacerbated in the second attempt. This should be a time for expression of appropriate appreciation, affirmation, pledges of prayer support, and closure.

If the call has been strong and the candidate declines, the committee will want to know why. This can be obtained by a closure conversation with the candidate. The committee can often learn much from a debriefing time with the minister. The committee should not become defensive or paranoid as a result of the rejection. Nor should the committee assume that all the pastor or staff minister says is correct. The committee must listen, learn, evaluate, and move on.

Should members of the committee resign? Only if somehow through the process the committee or certain members have become a source of division. Occasionally a member may have become disillusioned during the process, or outside circumstances will be a hindrance to the member's continuing. If a member resigns, he or she should be replaced by an alternate and the committee continue.

When a call has failed for whatever reason, the best action is to slow down, pray much, and revisit biographical profiles—including new ones received, retreat to the appropriate place in the process, and begin to move forward again. Hindsight will reveal that God was working even through this failed attempt. He will through it all work His best will (see Rom. 8:28). God will guide a prayerful committee to the right candidate, a call will be extended, and it will be accepted by the right person at the right time.

---

[1] Paul Nix, "On Seeing and Being Seen," *Church Administration*, July 1997, 24-8.

Chapter Eighteen

FOLLOWING THROUGH BEYOND THE ACCEPTED CALL

When a call has been extended and accepted, the major responsibility of a search committee is over; yet additional work must be done. Among the tasks the committee should either do themselves or request others to do are:

Notify all candidates.—It is rude for a committee to allow a minister with whom they have had some dealing to find out that he is no longer under consideration by reading a newspaper announcement that someone else has been called by the church. The committee should take the time to write a personal letter to each candidate, informing him that a minister has been called. In the letter mention the name of the minister, ask him to pray for your new pastor or staff minister and your church, thank him for his help, and assure him of the committee's prayers for him and his ministry. Those receiving these letters will appreciate your thoughtfulness. (Hopefully, if there were those on the committee's short list who accepted another ministry while under consideration by your committee, they were courteous enough to have notified you.)

Destroy any confidential information gathered on candidates other than the one called.—Often this material is sensitive in nature. The committee has a legal obligation and a Christian responsibility to make sure this information is not misused.

Return any material requested from candidates.—Tapes, biographical profiles, pictures, and similar material gathered should be destroyed if it is insignificant in value or returned if it is limited in number or cost is involved. In rare cases, a biographical profile on a candidate with whom the committee was impressed might be passed along to a similar church which is seeking a pastor or staff member. When this is done, do so discretely, if this would be acceptable to the minister involved. If in doubt, return the material to its source.

Look for opportunities to help your new pastor or staff minister.—The committee should make assignments among themselves to schedule calls (and call spontaneously) with various offers of help to the minister and his family. This is a time of anxiety for the minister's spouse and children. Look for ways to make the transition easy for them.

Help your new pastor or staff minister with housing needs.—If he is to move into a pastorium, work with the trustees and others to ensure that the house is spotlessly clean, newly painted, papered, and decorated. Involve the minister's wife in selecting colors, patterns, and decorating schemes. Respond positively to any reasonable requests to make the home personalized for its special new dwellers. Of course, the church should pay all expenses in preparing the home.

If the minister receives a housing allowance and will be purchasing his own home, (In most cases this is to everyone's advantage.) assist in enlisting the best help in expediting this matter. Give good advice as to areas where the minister's family will want to live. Introduce the family to suitable realtors. Be careful not to do this just for the benefit of a church member but for the benefit of the minister and his family. Help the minister connect with financial institutions. Many churches provide no-interest loans to help with a down payment in buying a house in the church's community. This is often a wonderful and helpful assistance.

When moving day arrives, arrange for women with the gift of hospitality and men with handyman abilities to help arrange furniture, hang pictures, provide food, and do anything and everything to make the move a good experience.

Make sure the church has arranged to pay all moving expenses.—If at all possible, the church should make the financial investment of paying professional movers. Remember that the household items of the minister's family represent a lifetime investment—financial and emotional. Often, churches pay expenses for a specified number of trips to house shop. Others reimburse real-estate fees involved in selling one's old house, utility hook-up fees, and expenses of licensing of automobiles (if an out-of-state move). A few churches give a predetermined amount of additional money to take care of incidental expenses for which the church requires no accounting. This is another one of those areas where it is best to err on the side of graciousness and generosity. Many of these items should have been spelled out in the pastor (or staff minister) and church agreement.

Help correlate plans for the first Sunday with the new minister and the congregation.—The first day of a new ministry is special. The new minister is in the spotlight. Mark this special day by promoting high attendance and a day of celebration.

Ask the new minister not to assume any pastoral duties until that first Sunday. This will give him opportunity to pray, study, and relax in preparation for this notable occasion. (For hints of how a new ministry should begin, read and give to your new minister the book *Surviving and Thriving in Today's Ministry*.)[1]

For a staff minister the first Sunday can be a wonderful time for the pastor to lead in an installation service that will give the pastor a forum to elevate the anticipated positive impact this minister of the gospel brings to the church. If the new minister is the pastor, allow him to determine the kind of program he desires for the first Sunday. Some pastors prefer to be installed by a visiting pastor friend or a denominational minister. Others would rather "hit the ground running" by preaching on this first Sunday. The advantage of the former is that of focusing on the relationship of the church with the association, state convention, or national convention. The advantage of the latter is that the pastor can immediately begin to build on the "honeymoon" spirit to set the direction of the church for the months and years to come.

Meet with the pastor to answer early questions and determine the formal close of the committee's ministry.—Many committees and ministers find it helpful to plan a meeting approximately 10 days after the minister's first Sunday. This informal meeting, led by the minister, will give him opportunity to ask questions and receive feedback from this group with whom he has, over a period of time, become comfortable. If some matters have not met the expectations of either party, this is often a time when situations can be rectified or clarified. If the minister is a staff minister, the pastor should also attend this meeting and lead the discussion.

The group can decide in this follow-up meeting when the search committee will conclude its assignment. A few ministers and committees find it helpful for this committee to continue for three to six months, meeting with the minister monthly or at his request in a similar fashion to that discussed in the previous paragraph.

Most churches still follow the procedure of bringing the search committee responsibilities to an immediate closure. This can be done appropriately on the following Sunday by introducing the committee to the congregation, presenting them with certificates of appreciation, and closing the committee's work with a prayer of thanksgiving.

A final responsibility of the search committee can be both an official and an unofficial function of the committee and individual members. This involves intentional actions of minister affirmation. The search committee chairman could ask the personnel committee chairman or chairman of deacons to plan an annual anniversary recognition time for the minister. Then members of the committee as church members should remain alert to opportunities to honor this minister and other ministers throughout the years.

---

[1] Don R. Mathis, *Surviving and Thriving in Today's Ministry* (Nashville: Convention Press, 1997). Available from the Customer Service Center, 1-800-458-2772.

Chapter Nineteen

CLOSING THOUGHTS FOR THE SEARCH COMMITTEE

- Before you begin each day as you continue the search process, ask God who He wants to be your new pastor or staff minister.
- Don't rush the process.
- Treat each minister with respect. You are dealing with men of God.
- Don't be hesitant to approach any minister to whom you feel led. Any true man of God will consider it an honor to be approached by any search committee.
- Don't expect the candidate to be just like the minister who just left your church. Each minister is called of God and uniquely gifted.
- Don't mislead a candidate. Be truthful. Answer questions that ought to be asked even if they aren't asked.
- Don't recommend a candidate to the church unless you can do so with conviction.
- Remain focused until God completes the process through you. Serving on a search committee is a tremendous responsibility, but an enormous sense of spiritual satisfaction will result from faithfulness in seeking and finding the will of God.

Appendix One

SCRIPTURES FOR COMMITTEE AND INDIVIDUAL STUDY

Passages relate to various aspects of the ministry—role, character, pay, confrontation, doctrine, as well as the various roles pastors and staff may have in the the life of a church. Some relevant Scriptures include:

- Deuteronomy 6:4-9
- Psalm 78:3-7; 127:3
- Matthew 18:3; 19:14; 28:19-20
- Mark 9:36-37; 10:14-15
- Luke 9:47-48; 18:16- 17
- Romans 12:6-8
- Ephesians 4:11-12
- Philippians 3:14
- 1 Thessalonians 2:11-12
- 1 Timothy 3:1-7; 4:1-16; 5:19-21; 6:31-21
- 2 Timothy 1:9; 2:1-7,14-16,22-26; 3:15-17; 4:1-5
- Titus 1:6-14; 2:1-15; 3:10
- 1 Peter 5:1-4
- 2 Peter 1:10
- 3 John 4

Appendix Two

A BIBLICAL FORMULA FOR CONFLICT RESOLUTION

Conflict is inevitable. It will emerge in a church fellowship. The following is a biblical formula for resolving such conflict.

The process.—If and when conflict occurs between the minister and the church, he is to be viewed and treated as a Christian brother and leader in accordance with 1 Timothy 5:19-20. Also, all of the principles of Matthew 5:23-25 and Matthew 18:15-17 apply to the minister as well as other church members.

This process of conflict resolution has four steps.

1. If your brother has something against you, go to him (see Matt. 5:23-25). If, on the other hand, your brother has wronged you, you go to him alone (see Matt. 18:15).

2. If your brother will not listen, take others with you (see Matt. 18:16).

3. If your brother will not listen, "tell it to the church" (Matt. 18:17). At this stage and for any subsequent action, outside help is advised.

4. If your brother will not listen to the church, "treat him as a heathen" (Matt. 18:17). This step is designed to motivate and bring him to reconciliation with God and the church.

The motive.—All redemptive solutions to conflict are motivated by love (see Eph. 4:15,29), with a desire for reconciliation (see Matt. 5:23-25) and healing that is bathed in prayer (see Jas. 5:16).

The temperament.—The basic temperament to be used in resolving conflict is found in the Golden Rule (see Luke 6:31; Matt. 7:12).

The results.—Broken relationships are mended, fellowship is deepened, and the church grows (see Acts 6:1-7).

The help.—Trained persons are available to assist and provide counsel to the church in developing a church covenant for solving conflict. At the invitation of the minister and church, a director of missions and/or a state convention leader will help. The church and minister are asked to pledge and follow an orderly process (see 1 Cor. 14:40) that will honor Christ.

Appendix Three

UNIQUE ISSUES AND SAMPLE JOB DESCRIPTIONS

JOB DESCRIPTION—SENIOR PASTOR

CALLING A MINISTER OF MUSIC

JOB DESCRIPTION—MINISTER OF MUSIC

CALLING A MINISTER OF EDUCATION

JOB DESCRIPTION—MINISTER OF EDUCATION

CALLING A MINISTER OF YOUTH

JOB DESCRIPTION—MINISTER OF YOUTH

CALLING A MINISTER OF PRESCHOOL/CHILDHOOD EDUCATION

JOB DESCRIPTION—
MINISTER OF PRESCHOOL OR CHILDHOOD EDUCATION

CALLING A MINISTER OF RECREATION

JOB DESCRIPTION—MINISTER OF RECREATION

CALLING A CHURCH BUSINESS ADMINISTRATOR

JOB DESCRIPTION—CHURCH BUSINESS ADMINISTRATOR

JOB DESCRIPTION—SENIOR PASTOR

Primary function.—To provide kingdom leadership to the members of this church enabling them to focus on the Great Commission, and equipping them to carry out the five functions of the New Testament church: evangelism, discipleship, ministry, fellowship, and worship.

RESPONSIBILITIES

Leading.—The senior pastor will lead and develop the pastoral team in equipping the congregation to fulfill the Great Commission and accomplish the purpose statement of this church. The senior pastor will lead and equip the body of deacons so they can effectively lead the ministry teams of the church.

Administering.—The senior pastor will provide direction and oversight to the administrative ministries of the church and will give leadership to the administrative ministries team of the congregation. The senior pastor will administer the pastoral team of this church.

Ministering.—The senior pastor will use his spiritual gifts to edify and build this local body of believers. The senior pastor will provide appropriate pastoral care to members of the church and the community and will equip the members of the pastoral team and the deacon body to do the same.

Communicating.—The senior pastor will preach and teach the Bible, believing that it has God for its author, salvation for its end, and truth without any mixture of error for its matter. The senior pastor will communicate the vision for ministry that God gives to this congregation.

EXPECTATIONS

The senior pastor is expected to be a servant leader. The senior pastor is expected to live an exemplary life modeling the call, character, and competencies becoming a minister of the gospel of Jesus Christ. The senior pastor will demonstrate a servant spirit as a growing disciple of Jesus Christ.

Source: Frank R. Lewis, *The Team Builder* (Nashville: Convention Press, 1997).

CALLING A MINISTER OF MUSIC

Here are some questions to consider when calling a minster of music:
- What worship style will be used?
- Is that style compatible with what the pastor desires?
- Is the person willing to try new, creative, and innovative worship ideas?
- Does the person know how to bring the people gathered for worship into the presence of the Lord?
- Does the person have a good platform personality?
- Is the person a good musician?
- Can he/she effectively lead and organize the music ministry of the church?
- Does he/she walk with the Lord?

Many times a church will call someone that is not compatible with the pastor. The individual may have a different philosophy of worship or may not be willing to get out of his or her comfort zone. When I have the opportunity to visit with committees who are searching for a minister of music, I encourage them to sit down with the pastor to see what he desires. Life is too short to call someone who is not going the same direction as the pastor.

The music search committee should consider some other important areas. What worship standards or goals for the worship services will the prospective minister of music try to achieve? A music committee might want to consider the following "worship standards and goals":

1. Focus on the Lord Jesus Christ. Bringing focus to worship means that the music, drama, and other spoken parts of the service will all move toward the central theme of the service. A unified theme helps to focus our worship on the Lord Jesus Christ.

2. Worship God "in Spirit and in truth." Each person who holds a microphone or leads in worship in any way in the service should communicate with integrity and genuine emotion. Their testimonies for Christ should be true and in no way a stumbling block for others.

3. Include the following three phases of worship in every worship service:
   - Praise.—Person to person, we encourage one another to worship celebratively!
   - Praise.—Person to God, we sing songs and speak Scripture directly to God, intimately.

- Worship.—God to person, we open our hearts and minds to receive God's Word.

4. Use methods and formats that are relevant to lost people today.

5. Honor God with excellence.

6. Involve each member of the congregation in corporate worship.

Two other important areas to consider are worship planning and creating a worship script. The trend in worship is for a team of individuals to be involved in the planning of the worship services directed and led by the minister of music. Is this compatible with the direction the pastor wants to go? It is important for the minister of music to be well organized. He or she must be capable of leading a group of individuals in planning worship.

Last, but not least, is the candidate a musician only or also a minister? Churches today are looking for those who are ministers first and musicians second.

Source: Robert R. Wagoner, large church worship consultant, Music Ministries Department, Sunday School Board, Nashville, Tennessee.

JOB DESCRIPTION—MINISTER OF MUSIC

(This job description serves as a sample of duties that may be assigned to the minister of music. Each church will adapt this model to fit the needs of the congregation and the minister.)

Principle function.—The minister of music is responsible to the church and the pastor for developing and promoting the music ministry of the church.

RESPONSIBILITIES

1. Direct the organization and implementation of a comprehensive church music program including choir, vocal and/or instrumental ensembles, and drama teams.
2. Assist the pastor in planning congregational services of the church and be responsible for selecting the music.
3. Serve as a leader in the worship services, giving direction to the congregational singing, choir, and other phases of worship.
4. Direct major service choirs and other choirs or ensembles as personal schedule will permit.
5. Supervise the work of paid music staff workers and volunteers. Conduct regular staff meetings for the purpose of evaluation and planning.
6. Cooperate with the church nominating committee to enlist and train leaders for the church music ministry as well as song leaders and accompanists for church educational organizations.
7. Serve as member of the Church Council or church leadership team. Coordinate the music program with the organizational calendar and emphases of the church.
8. Lead in maintaining a church music committee, team, or council. Seek input from members in matters such as goal setting, evaluation, leadership, personnel policies for paid staff, facilities, finance, and administrative procedures.
9. Serve on, and work with, church committees as assigned.
10. Plan, organize, and promote concerts, choir tours, mission trips, retreats, festivals, workshops, clinics, and other special programs to enhance the music ministry.
11. Oversee maintenance of the music library, materials, supplies, musical instruments, and other equipment useful in the music ministry.

12. Prepare reports necessary to keep the church fully informed concerning the music ministry.

13. Prepare, with assistance from the music committee and music staff members, an annual music budget reflecting the needs of the entire music program. Administrate the budget once it is approved by the church.

14. Be informed of denominational goals, emphases, publications, materials, policies, and plans for employing them as they relate to the local church. Cooperate with associational and state leaders in promoting activities of mutual interest.

15. Assist other staff members in churchwide events when needed.

16. Assist in the selection and provision of appropriate music for weddings, funerals, special projects, and other church-related activities.

17. Give direction to, and participate in, a plan of visitation and enlistment.

18. Visit hospitals and assist in pastoral care when called upon.

19. Keep informed on current music methods, materials, promotional ideas, and administrative techniques.

20. Maintain a consistent program of self-improvement.

CALLING A MINISTER OF EDUCATION

The heart of the issue for the church and for the minister of education is in both placing their priorities in the proper perspective. The priority should be God first, family second, church third. Pastors, committee members and leaders, and staff—including the minister of education can easily get these priorities out of sequence.

Prior to a call from a church to the minister of education should come real clarity of priority. Misunderstandings often lead to frustration for all involved. That can easily be avoided by discussing each of these three areas.

1. What is expected in the area of personal, spiritual growth and development?
2. What is expected in taking time to spend with family, days off, vacations, and time spent attending professional development seminars, etc.?
3. What is expected in relation to work? Office hours, days off, holidays, and other work-related issues should be clearly outlined and discussed before the prospective minister of education ever begins to work on the field.

These areas should be carefully discussed in relation to the expectations of the church, the pastor, and the new staff member. Clarity is essential if the ministry is going to enjoy long tenure and lasting ministry impact.

Assessing someone's work is not an easy task because often assessments are more subjective than objective. However, with the minister of education, you have many opportunities to evaluate the work he or she has done. You can ask such questions as:

- What do Sunday School attendance and enrollment figures indicate?
- How many new persons have been enlisted in ministry positions?
- How many new units have been started?
- What are the results of weekly or monthly visitation emphases?
- What kind of training has been done to enlist and develop lay leaders for the many educational positions available in the church.
- What personal and professional development has been taking place? What conferences, seminars, and retreats has the minister of education attended?
- What religious education organizations does the prospective staff member attend or hold membership in?
- What books has this person read in the last 6-12 months?
- What communication skills are evident in issues of the church newsletter or various publications for which the new minister of education has written?

- What do committee chairpersons or team leaders say about the effectiveness of the perspective minister of education in leading meetings and training lay leaders to facilitate educational meetings?
- Does this person work well with lay leaders?
- If you have a multi-person staff, what history does this new staff person have in relating to existing staff?
- Is the candidate a team player?

INTERVIEWING A PERSPECTIVE MINISTER OF EDUCATION

All inquiries and contacts prior to coming to the potential church field should be handled by the appropriate committee within the church. In many churches this is the personnel committee. However, in some churches, the pastor has been given the task of finding the right person to work on the team. In other churches, a special educational task force or team has been developed and charged with bringing the right person to the church field.

Once the candidate is on the field for either an unofficial or official visit, the church might want to consider the following:

- Give the person a tour of the community.
- Make sure the person sees the entire church campus, inside and out.
- Be sure the educational records are at the disposal of the prospective minister of education. This person may want to spend considerable time looking at the past track record of the different educational organizations for at least the past year and perhaps the past two to five years.
- Meet with the personnel committee or the group charged with bringing this staff person on board.
- Meet with the pastor and staff.
- Meet with the leaders of different educational organizations.
- Meet with a few key leaders from the church who have not been on any formal committee interviewing the prospective minister of education.

Not all staff persons and/or ministers of education feel comfortable or adequate preaching. However, the prospective minister of education should be prepared to share his or her testimony during the worship experience.

Source: Ron Pratt is a consultant, Pastor-Staff Leadership Department, Sunday School Board, Nashville, Tennessee.

JOB DESCRIPTION—MINISTER OF EDUCATION

The minister of education is responsible to the pastor for providing staff leadership to the entire church educational program.

RESPONSIBILITIES

1. Determine the purpose of and the organizational structure for each educational organization, program, ministry, or emphasis. Examples include Sunday School, Discipleship Training, missions education, small-group studies, Vacation Bible School, church media, etc.

2. Use or establish a key lay leadership organization or organizations to plan, coordinate, and evaluate the effectiveness of the various educational ministries. These lay leader organizations may include Church Council, Sunday School Council, Discipleship Training Council, Missions Education Council, educational leadership/development team, lead teams to manage individual programs, etc.

3. Believing that every Christian is gifted and those gifts are to build up the body of Christ, the church, seek to enlist and train people to serve God, using their giftedness, in various areas of educational ministry. This might mean using a nominating committee or other standing committee. It might mean that the staff will enlist leaders, or it could mean that a separate leadership enlistment team is established to manage the enlistment process for the various educational ministries.

4. Develop special training opportunities for educational leaders including all age-group leaders serving in various educational ministries. These annual training sessions might include Vacation Bible School training, outreach/evangelism training, teaching-learning training, etc.

5. Develop the appropriate budgets to ensure the physical and financial resources for developing and expanding Christian educational ministries.

6. Lead the church to evaluate and select the most appropriate curriculum for each of the educational ministries.

7. Serve on the Church Council or leadership team.

8. Help plan, coordinate, conduct, and evaluate the worship services as requested.

9. Supervise appropriate church staff members, such as age-group staff, office staff, custodial staff, etc., as assigned by the pastor and/or church.

10. Join in a network of other professional educators to continue to enhance your personal and professional development in Christian education.

CALLING A MINISTER OF YOUTH

Several factors are unique to calling a minister of youth. These include appropriate age, love for teenagers, and ability to coordinate and lead.

Appropriate age.—A decade or two ago, most churches just assumed they would call a youth minster as close in age to the teenagers as possible. The feeling was that teenagers would relate best to a person who only recently had also been a teenager.

In the present era of youth ministry, leaders in their younger twenties continue to be effective in youth ministry. Even so, a growing number of churches now understand that leaders in their thirties, forties, and even beyond can coordinate effective youth ministries.

Youth ministers relate to three primary audiences: teenagers, parents of teenagers, and adults who serve in youth ministry. Age is a definite plus when giving leadership to parents and adult leaders. At the same time, age doesn't have to be a negative when relating to the teenagers themselves.

More than anything, teenagers today need unconditional love, unconditional acceptance, affirmation, consistency, and godly role modeling. Youth ministers three times the age of youth can offer each of these qualities.

In addition, experienced leaders often have stronger skills in counseling and crisis intervention and in planning and administration. Search committees would do well to consider candidates of all ages as they seek God's person for youth ministry.

Love for teenagers.—Youth ministry requires a number of skills and competencies. The presence or absence of those skills helps determine the degree of effectiveness in ministry. Fortunately, most of those skills can be learned through both formal and continuing education. One quality, though, cannot be taught by any school or reading plan. An effective youth minister absolutely must have a deep love for teenagers.

Teenagers have an uncanny ability to detect the motives behind adult involvement in their lives. A church youth program will never prosper unless the teenagers can sense their key leader has an unconditional love for them that drives all he or she does. As search committee members consider a potential candidate, they must look for a core love for youth that goes far beyond salary or ego.

Ability to coordinate and lead.—Youth ministry in the past was often led by a person who enjoyed doing it all himself. That approach to leadership has become outdated. Churches need youth ministers who call out the gifts and abilities of many parents, leaders, and teenagers. Youth ministers simply cannot micromanage the planning and executing of every youth event and at the same time be a visionary, coordinator, trainer, crisis counselor, motivator, and so on.

As search committee members interview candidates, they need to listen for those who have a specific plan for coordinating many adults and key youth who will take on specific leadership roles in ministry. Equipping and then releasing the "saints" to do the work of the ministry is absolutely essential in contemporary youth ministry.

Source: Richard Ross is youth ministry consultant, Pastor-Staff Leadership Department, Sunday School Board, Nashville, Tennessee.

JOB DESCRIPTION—MINISTER OF YOUTH

(This job description serves as a sample of duties that may be assigned to the minister of youth. Each church will adapt this model to fit the needs of the congregation and the minister.)

Principle function.—The minister of youth is called by God to follow Christ in a life of discipleship, using the leadership gifts given by the Holy Spirit to lead the church in carrying out the Great Commission for the purpose of expanding the kingdom of God.

RESPONSIBILITIES
The minister of youth will:

Minister
- Serve as an integral member of the pastoral ministries team and give full support to the leadership role of the senior pastor.
- Provide pastoral ministry with the youth ministry family (youth, parents of youth, and youth leaders), and coordinate the training of others to do likewise.

Administer
- Coordinate the weekly youth education organizations. In cooperation with the minister of education, coordinate an overall youth curriculum plan for the church, leading to properly sequenced, balanced, and comprehensive Christian education for youth active in the youth organization for six years.
- Coordinate the creation of the annual youth ministry budget proposal and administer that budget as approved by the budget planning committee.
- Coordinate programming and events for parents of youth related to their parenting roles and events for parents and youth.
- Coordinate space utilization in youth ministry and make recommendations concerning building and remodeling needs.
- Assist the youth organizations in providing opportunities for members of the youth ministry family to be directly involved in missions and ministry, both locally and away.
- Coordinate the training and mentoring of members of the youth ministry family who sense a call to ministry vocations.
- Coordinate planning to ensure Christian youth experience authentic worship

personally, with the youth group, and with the full church body.

- Coordinate planning to ensure youth experience true fellowship within the body of Christ.

Lead

- Guide the youth ministry family to define, communicate, and implement its purpose, vision, and strategy.
- Represent youth ministry on the Church Council or church leadership team and with other church groups as called on.
- Chair the Youth Ministry Council. Guide the development of the youth ministry calendar, and coordinate youth ministry lead teams.
- Coordinate the enlisting, discipling, training, and motivating of adults to serve in youth ministry in cooperation with the nominating committee.
- Fine-tune skills in leading, administering, ministering, and communicating through a structured reading plan, high-quality conferences, and formal education.
- Share the gospel with lost youth and lost parents on an ongoing basis, both individually and corporately.
- Coordinate an overall youth evangelism strategy for the church, ensure evangelism is a goal of all youth programming, and coordinate continuing training in soul-winning for all members of the youth ministry family.
- Network with other evangelical youth leaders in the community to support youth in starting and strengthening school campus ministries and to coordinate events designed to evangelize and disciple youth.
- Coordinate the training of youth to serve as missionaries on their school campuses.
- As allowed by law, minister on secondary school campuses within the sphere of influence of the church.
- Coordinate youth ministry communication and promotion plans in concert with lead teams, youth organizations, and pastoral ministers.

ACCOUNTABILITY

The minister of youth reports to the minister of education (or pastor) and supervises interns and volunteer youth staff.

CALLING A MINISTER
OF PRESCHOOL/CHILDHOOD EDUCATION

When seeking the right person to lead the church's ministry of preschool or childhood education, the church must reflect on how it views and values children. Is there an awareness of the pressures children experience today, an understanding of how children learn, the importance of Christian role models? The church must recognize the need to minister to the "total child" and seek a person with the personal characteristics and expertise to do so.

The minister of childhood education is to be a growing Christian, practicing regular Bible study and devotional times. He or she should be enthusiastic about sharing a personal testimony about God's working in his or her life.

Formal education for childhood ministry may be acquired through college and seminary. A major study of preschool and elementary education seems logical. Minors in psychology, counseling, journalism, drama, and art are good choices. The experience of student teaching is valuable, even if it requires working toward a teaching certificate. Most seminaries offer programs with an emphasis in childhood religious education. If possible, prospective ministers of childhood education should attend seminary and earn a master's degree in religious education. Seminary experiences should be coupled with practical experience in a local church. A planned program of continuing education can occur at conference centers, local workshops, and seminary continuing education seminars. The minister of childhood education should search out educational experiences and take advantage of as many as possible.

The minister of preschool or childhood education should work to present a positive image in the church. This can be done as he/she is willing to become actively involved in all facets of church life—not just the required area of work. Church members will identify positively with ministers who are willing to teach children, work in extended session, participate in visitation, attend worship services, and join in fellowship with other adults. If possible, the minister of childhood education should participate regularly in the church's worship services in some visible way.

The effectiveness of the work of a minster of preschool or childhood education begins from within and becomes a way of life, a state of being.

Source: Adapted from Marcie Creech, *The Ministry of Childhood Education, Revised* (Nashville: Convention Press, 1990).

JOB DESCRIPTION—MINISTER OF PRESCHOOL OR CHILDHOOD EDUCATION

(This job description serves as a sample of duties that may be assigned to the minister of preschool or childhood education. Each church will adapt this model to fit the needs of the congregation and the minister.)

Principle function.—The minister of preschool or childhood education is responsible to the minister of education for assisting church program organizations in developing a comprehensive program of childhood education, including planning, coordination, evaluation, and education. The minister consults with other staff members concerning activities, policies, and procedures that relate to their areas.

RESPONSIBILITIES

1. Work in cooperation with appropriate persons, including the nominating committee, in selecting, enlisting, training, and counseling with preschool and children's workers in the church program organizations.
2. Conduct special training projects focused on education and motivation for preschool and children's workers.
3. Conduct meetings as needed or when appropriate for parents of preschoolers and children.
4. Advise in the use of program materials, equipment, supplies, and space by preschool and children's groups in all church program organizations.
5. Work with the minister of music, director of the church media library, and the minister of recreation to provide needed services.
6. Assist with planning and conducting special projects and activities (such as camps, retreats, and fellowships) for preschoolers and children.
7. Maintain an active program of personal witnessing and ministry.
8. Work with organizational leaders to coordinate visitation for the Preschool and Children's Divisions.
9. Work with program leaders and teachers and appropriate staff members to resolve philosophical, procedural, and scheduling problems in the Preschool and Children's Divisions.
10. Prepare and administer the annual childhood education budget according to church policy.

11. Be informed of denominational goals, emphases, publications, materials, and plans for using them as they relate to the local church and its programs.

12. Keep informed on current early childhood and elementary education methods, materials, promotional ideas, and administrative techniques, using them where appropriate.

13. Perform other duties as requested by the supervisor.

CALLING A MINISTER OF RECREATION

An effective minister of recreation will possess the following qualities.

1. Be a committed Christian who leads a balanced life.
2. Have a call to recreation ministry.
3. Have a vision to use recreation as a ministry tool.
4. Have an undergraduate degree in recreation or related field.
5. Have earned a seminary degree (preferred).
6. Have good people skills—able to relate to all ages.
7. Have good planning, organizing, and communication skills.
8. Have a fundamental knowledge of business practices.
9. Be able to work in a hectic, off-hours environment.
10. Be willing to try new things.
12. Have the "big picture" of what the church is and how it ministers.

The minister of recreation does not need to be an athlete.

Source: John Garner is director, Church Recreation Program, Pastor-Staff Leadership Department, Sunday School Board, Nashville, Tennessee.

JOB DESCRIPTION—MINISTER OF RECREATION

Principle function.—The minister of recreation is responsible to the minister of education for leading the church in planning, conducting, and evaluating a program of recreation for church members and other persons in the community.

RESPONSIBILITIES

1. Direct the planning, coordination, conducting, and evaluation of recreation activities in the church.
2. Coordinate and administer activities in the church's recreation or family life center, as assigned by the church.
3. Work with the church nominating committee to recruit and enlist workers for the church's recreation program.
4. Plan and coordinate training for all volunteer recreation workers in relationship to the Discipleship Training program.
5. Serve as ex officio member of the Church Council or leadership team and coordinate the recreation activities with the calendar and emphases of the church.
6. Serve as recreation resource person and adviser to organizations of the church as requested.
7. Lead the church to provide equipment and supplies needed in the recreation activities.
8. Supervise the inventory, care, repair, and storage of recreation equipment and supplies.
9. Provide representation for the church in planning, conducting, and evaluating recreation activities that involve other churches and groups.

Source: Adapted from Tim J. Holcomb, *Personnel Administration Guide for Southern Baptist Churches* (Nashville: Convention Press, 1988).

CALLING A CHURCH BUSINESS ADMINISTRATOR

Roger Skelton wrote that there are three primary purposes of administration:

1. To help the church be the redemptive, covenant body Christ intended.

2. To enable the church to be increasingly effective in carrying out its mission.

3. To manage the affairs of the congregation as expeditiously as possible.[1]

The complex issues that face the church today often require that the church call a business administrator to give oversight to the administrative functions that enable the church to minister effectively.

Some churches will call a skilled administrator from within their congregation. Others will implement a search process outside the congregation. In either case, the candidate for church business administrator must exhibit a sense of call to use his or her expertise within the realm of the church's life and ministry. Management education and experience, with an understanding of the issues unique to nonprofit organizations, will benefit the administrator. In addition to the demonstration of administrative expertise, the church business administrator must:

1. Understand the mission and purpose of the church.

2. Identify his or her role as manager-minister.

3. Optimize human, physical, information, and financial resources.

4. Apply the five functions of the management process—planning, organizing, staffing, directing, and controlling.

5. Exhibit integrity and high ethical standards in his or her personal and professional life.

Source: Adapted from Marvin Myers, *Managing the Business Affairs of the Church* (Nashville: Convention Press, 1981).

---

[1] Roger Skelton, "The Meaning and Ministry of Administration in a Church," *Search* (Winter 1974), 23-30.

JOB DESCRIPTION—
CHURCH BUSINESS ADMINISTRATOR

Principle function.—To assist the church in carrying out its mission by planning and implementing effective organizational and fiscal processes to achieve its goals.

RESPONSIBILITIES

1. Work with paid staff and church members to achieve the goals of the church.
2. Establish and operate an efficient plan of financial record keeping and reporting; develop bookkeeping procedures.
3. Prepare financial information for the finance and budget committees and treasurer of the church.
4. Serve as resource person regarding legal and business matters of the church. Study annually the church's insurance and recommend change if needed.
5. Develop and implement a long-range plan for updating equipment, furnishings, and software.
6. Lead the staff in acquiring training in ministry and technical skills.
7. Maintain records on church staff personnel. Establish and maintain records of equipment and facilities. Approve and process requisitions and purchase orders.
8. Administer church-adopted policies and procedures concerning the use of all church properties and facilities.
9. Assist the church property and space committee in working with architect, contractors, and others in building, remodeling, and equipping church buildings.
10. Serve on the Church Council or leadership team. Serve as ex officio member of the deacons and church committees/teams.
11. Work with the church property and space committee in preparing an annual budget of maintenance and equipment needs.
12. Supervise workers in the maintenance and repair of all physical properties. Establish and implement cleaning, painting, and renovating schedules. Operate within approved budget.
13. Supervise the operation of food services.
14. Supervise assigned office personnel.

Source: Adapted from Tim J. Holcomb, *Personnel Administration Guide for Southern Baptist Churches* (Nashville: Convention Press, 1988).

Appendix Four

LIST OF SAMPLE FORMS INCLUDED IN THE ELECTRONIC APPENDIX

Samples of the following forms and documents can be found in the electronic appendix in the *Pastor and Staff Search Committee Kit* (ISBN #0-7673-9120-9), compiled by Don R. Mathis and Donna J. Gandy. The kit is available by calling 1-800-458-4772 or from your Baptist Book Store or LifeWay Christian Store.

ELECTRONIC APPENDIX

(3.5" diskette. Documents are in customizable Microsoft Word, WordPerfect, and text files.)

1. Congregational Survey
2. Church and Community Profile
3. Supply Preaching Form
4. Preaching/Video Viewing Guide
5. Sample Letters
   • To potential candidates
   • To persons listed as references
6. Sample Candidate Interview Questions
7. Sample Reference Interview Questions

9. Release of Confidential Information Form

10. Glossary of Academic Degrees

11. Compensation Worksheet

12. Agreement Between Minister and Congregation

13. Installation Service

14. Ministerial Job Descriptions

The Kit also includes a mini-training conference for your committee on audiocassette: A charge to the committee from Dr. Gene Mims, vice president, Church Growth Group, Sunday School Board; and an interview with Dr. Don Mathis, director, Pastor-Staff Leadership Department, Sunday School Board, and author of *The Pastor and Staff Search Committee Guide.*